SDI Computer Nitrox Diving
second edition

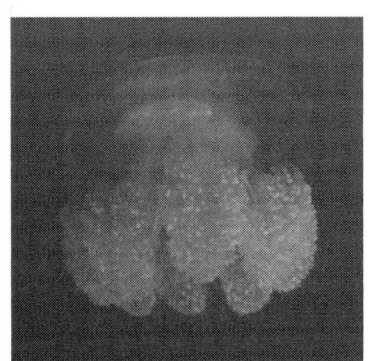
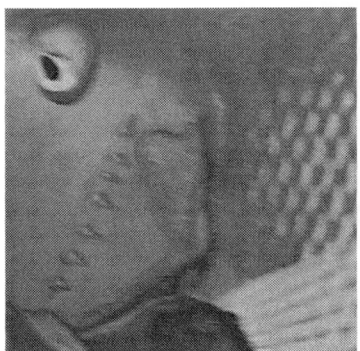

Computer Nitrox Diver

Publisher:
International Training
Phone: 888-778-9073 Fax: 207-729-4453
tdisdi.com   Email: worldhq@tdisdi.com

© **International Training 2013**   v.0221

Executive Editor
Brian Carney

Editor
Steve Lewis

Contributors
Harry Averill
Steven Barsky

Photography by
Doug Arnberg
Harry Averill
Aaron Bruce
Flemming Elleboe
Bret Gilliam
Sean Harrison

Trademarks

Scuba Diving International®, Technical Diving International® and Emergency Response Diving International® are registered trademarks of International Training. Viton® is a registered trademark of Dupont Dow Elastomers. Ziploc® is a registered trademark of SC Johnson & Son, Inc.

Notice of Rights:

All rights reserved. No part of this book may be reproduced or transmitted in any form by any means, electronic, mechanical, photocopying, recording, or otherwise without the prior written permission of the publisher. For information on getting permission for reprints and excerpts, contact Scuba Diving International.

ISBN: 1-931451-28-1   Item#: 210001-01

WARNING

Nitrox diving is an activity in which divers use breathing gases that contain elevated levels of oxygen, beyond the 21 percent found in normal air. There are risks in Nitrox diving that go beyond the usual risks associated with recreational scuba diving.

Although this book was written specifically for an instructional course devoted to using Nitrox mixtures containing up to and including 40 percent oxygen, it is understood that people make mistakes and misunderstand each other. For this reason, anyone who uses Nitrox must be aware of the special risks to which one is exposed when using breathing mixtures with elevated levels of oxygen.

Breathing gas mixtures that contain more than 40 percent oxygen are subject to fires and explosions if improperly handled. Although this course material is designed to train divers who will use mixtures containing up to and including 40 percent oxygen, as a Nitrox diver, you may be exposed to these risks by having your cylinders filled at a Nitrox facility or by being in the vicinity of other divers who are using mixtures that contain greater than 40 percent oxygen

Any time a diver uses Nitrox under water there are also additional risks including temporary visual and hearing disturbances, irritability, nausea, dizziness, and convulsions. Visual and hearing disturbances and irritability can lead a person to make incorrect choices in an emergency situation. Nausea and dizziness can lead to vomiting underwater, which can lead to drowning and death. Convulsions underwater almost always lead to drowning and death. Although these risks are small when using Nitrox containing up to and including 40 percent oxygen (EAN40), every diver must be aware of and know how to avoid these risks. This book is designed to provide information to help the diver avoid these problems.

CONTENTS

Introduction **9**
    Guide to Symbols 13

Chapter 1   **This is Nitrox** **14**
    Knowledge Quest 20

Chapter 2   **How Nitrox Works to Give You More Bottom Time** **22**
    Knowledge Quest 36

Chapter 3   **Risks Associated with Nitrox Diving** **38**
    Knowledge Quest 47

Chapter 4   **Selecting Equipment for Nitrox Diving** ... **48**
    Knowledge Quest 61

Chapter 5   **Filling Your Cylinders with Nitrox** **62**
    Knowledge Quest 71

Chapter 6   **Planning the Nitrox Dive** **72**
    Knowledge Quest 81

Chapter 7   **Extending Your Nitrox Knowledge** **82**
    Knowledge Quest 87

Appendices **88**
    Appendix I: Glossary 89
    Appendix II: Tables 105
    Appendix III: An Introduction to Dive Computers .. 113

 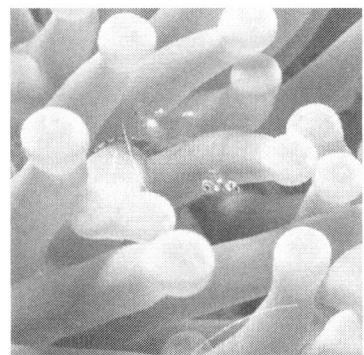 

INTRODUCTION

Congratulations. You are about to join the special group of divers who have chosen to invest in continuing education. You will not regret it. In fact, this SDI specialty course will change the way you think about diving and the way you execute your dives.

Few advances in the realm of diving have had a more profound impact during the past two decades than the widespread availability of Enriched Air Nitrox. And nothing has made the switch from diving air to diving its more exotic cousin more straightforward or more enjoyable than Nitrox programmable dive computers.

Simply put, nitrox – air with additional oxygen content – allows divers to enjoy longer bottom times (and shorter surface intervals) than their air-breathing dive buddies, while staying within the limits that were stressed in their open water training.

Nitrox makes this possible because it contains reduced levels of nitrogen compared to air and less nitrogen translates into more bottom time! But of course there is a price to pay. Diving nitrox does present risks that are not present diving air, and these risks require that divers to take some additional steps during their pre-dive planning and then adhere to that dive plan.

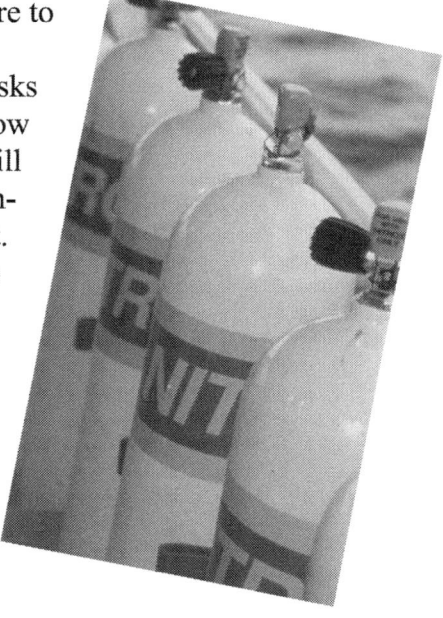

During this course, you will learn about all the risks associated with Nitrox diving and the rules to follow to make sure those risks will be avoided. You will also learn how to dive safely with Nitrox mixes containing oxygen levels ranging from 22 to 40 percent.

In addition, you will learn that the best tool to help you apply your new-found knowledge and to help you track your nitrox dives thoroughly is your nitrox programmable dive computer. (Don't worry if you are coming into this SDI specialty class without the basic understanding of how to dive with a computer. You will find a comprehensive introduction to dive computers in the appendix section of this manual.)

You will discover that diving Nitrox is not rocket science. The concepts are straightforward and easy to understand. Of course, like most things relating to diving, the subject does have another side; and, if the science and technology behind the basic concepts of nitrox interest you or if you find yourself wondering how nitrox with higher levels of oxygen than 40 percent would affect your diving, you may want to consider continuing on to Technical Diving International's (TDI's) Advanced Nitrox Diver course.

Good luck and dive safe and dive often; the underwater world is waiting for you.

Dive Often - Dive Safe

Brian Carney   *Steve Lewis*

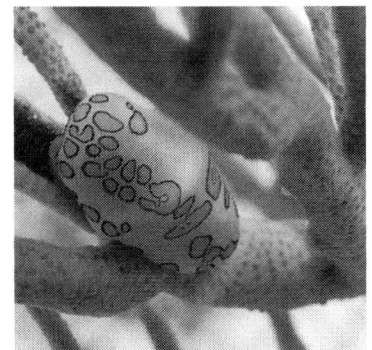

Guide to Symbols

This manual uses a variety of symbols to identify the type of information you will be reading. These include:

Learn by Example
Following many of the step-by-step procedures described in this manual, you will find a practical example of how these procedures are applied. These are identified by the *Learn by Example* symbol.

Find Out More
The *Find Out More* symbol identifies information that will tell you what SDI/TDI publications or courses will allow you to learn more about related subject matter.

Caution
The *Caution* symbol identifies information that may be critical to your health, safety and well being.

Scuba IQ Review
At the end of each chapter, you'll find questions that test your knowledge of what you have previously read. These are identified by the *Scuba IQ Review* symbol.

chapter one

1

This is Nitrox...
A simple to understand and user-friendly gas!

In this chapter, you'll learn about:
- What Nitrox is and its benefits
- How to use Nitrox

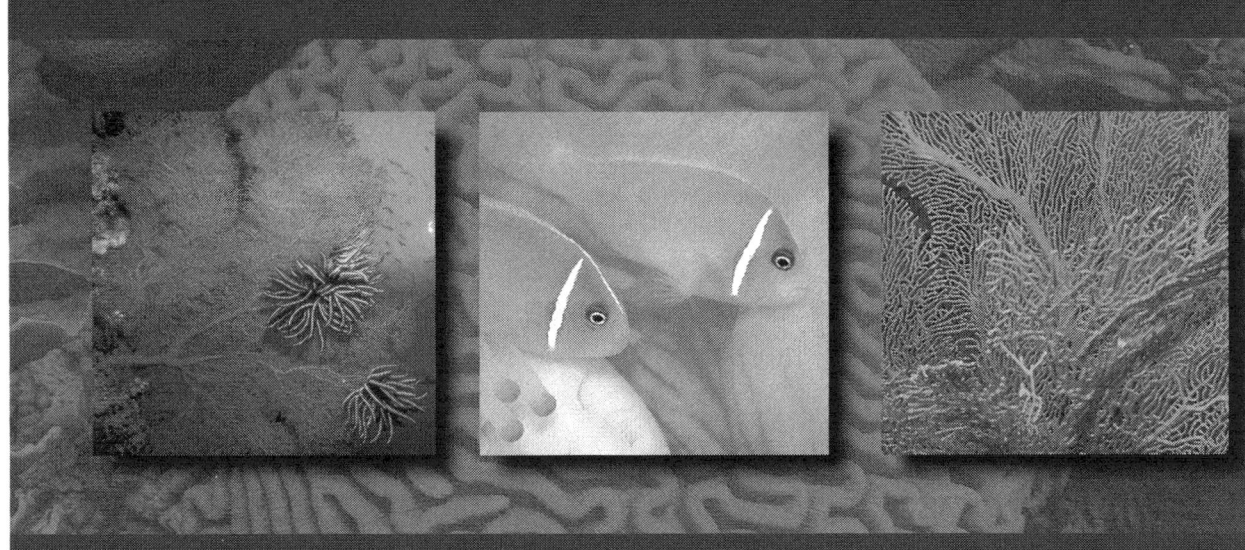

The really fun part of diving is all about being underwater. That's what we train for; that's what we look forward to, and that's what we talk about with our friends. But most of us would agree that our dives seem to be over much too soon, and surface intervals seem to drag on forever.

Of course, we could extend our bottom time way past the recommended no decompression limits and execute staged decompression diving! But for most of us, the additional training, equipment and dedication necessary to properly plan and execute technical dives presents too much of a commitment. Is there a simpler alternative? Luckily there is: Nitrox allows sport divers like you and your buddies to extend your bottom times and to shorten your surface intervals significantly compared to your previous air dives.

You've probably heard of nitrox, and you have probably seen stickers on tanks, dive bags and log books advertising its presence. In all likelihood, you have also heard it referred to by a variety of names: enriched air, oxygen enriched air, SafeAir™, Denitrogenated Air™, EAN, EANx, NOAA Nitrox I or NOAA Nitrox II. When SDI first began teaching sport divers to dive with nitrox, the jokers in dive shops and on charter boats also sometimes called it "voodoo gas," harking back to the days when some scuba organizations were reluctant to accept diving with Nitrox into the mainstream of their curriculum – a practice now thankfully in the distant past.

Regardless of the name, it is important to know that all of these terms refer to the same thing – i.e., nitrox – a mix of nitrogen and oxygen just like air. However, unlike air ,which normally contains approximately 79% nitrogen and 21% oxygen, nitrox contains a higher percentage of oxygen.

> *Nitrox allows sport divers to significantly extend bottom times and shorten surface intervals.*

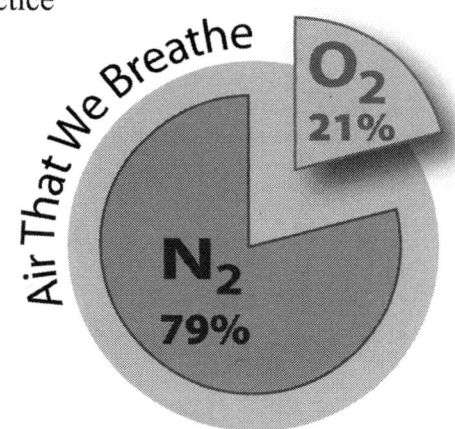

Chapter 1 | This is Nitrox... A simple to understand and user-friendly gas.

The percentage of oxygen contained in a nitrox mix can be varied according to the diver's individual needs, and we'll discuss what those needs might be as we work our way through this text, but with an SDI nitrox card you can walk into a dive store, and get any mix containing any percentage of oxygen from 22% to 40%. That is as long as the dive center offers nitrox and has a trained "nitrox blender" on staff!

Nitrogen and oxygen can be mixed in any ratio, but some commonly used mixtures include:
- EAN32 = 68% nitrogen, 32% oxygen
- EAN36 = 64% nitrogen, 36% oxygen
- EAN30 = 70% nitrogen, 30 % oxygen

When you dive using nitrox you can take advantage of two major benefits. The first is that you can increase your maximum allowable bottom time. This happens because the extra oxygen added to your breathing gas has displaced nitrogen. Because there is less nitrogen in the mix to be absorbed by your body, you can spend longer at depth before you reach the nitrogen limit – which is the decompression limit. Secondly, since you are absorbing less nitrogen on a given dive, your surface intervals can usually be shortened.

You will see that the most efficient way to dive nitrox is to let a special nitrox dive computer track bottom time and allowable surface intervals for you; however, another way that divers use nitrox is to dive with nitrox, but use a dive computer designed for air diving and follow the air diving times and surface intervals calculated by their computer. This method is considered very conservative from the DCS management standpoint and is sometimes used by older divers who are not in the greatest shape, or divers who have suffered from decompression sickness. The thinking is that by using nitrox in

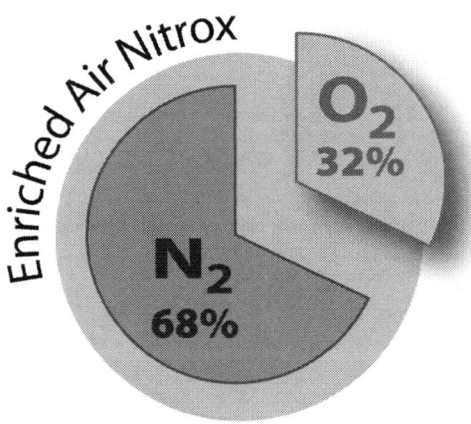

this way, they improve their chances of avoiding decompression sickness. While many divers and medical experts believe that this concept is probably correct, there have been no scientific tests to prove this theory.

You will be able to dive nitrox without making any marked changes in your diving !

Some divers also think that by using nitrox they suffer from less fatigue after diving. Others believe that by using nitrox they will be less susceptible to nitrogen narcosis at depth. There have been no scientific tests to prove or disprove either of these claims. With a little experience, you will form your own opinion and since both narcosis and post dive fatigue are greatly influenced by one's mental state, your opinion will be valid… for you!

In all likelihood you'll find that diving with nitrox does not make you feel any differently underwater than breathing ordinary compressed air. And in most respects, you will be able to dive with nitrox without making any marked changes in your diving. Essentially, most things that must change have more to do with dive planning than dive execution.

When you dive with nitrox, it is essential that you track your exposure to increased levels of oxygen. When your dive computer is properly set for the oxygen mixture you are using, it will monitor your oxygen exposure and decompression status automatically. In addition, you will have to pay particular attention to your maximum depth, because each nitrox mixture has a maximum operating depth (MOD) beyond which it must not be used. You'll learn more about this in the next chapter.

If one does dive at the MOD of a particular nitrox mixture, the oxygen time limit for a single dive is 45 minutes. If one backs off a little from this exposure, the single dive time limit increases dramatically. Also, over the course of a 24-hour period, you will have a cumulative time limit for oxygen exposure at the maximum operating depth of two and a half hours in any 24-hour period. With most dive computers, you will reach your no-decompression limits before you ever experience a limitation due to your oxygen exposure. This exposure to higher levels of oxygen carries a certain level of risk, similar to the level of risk of decompression sickness. This will be explained in further detail in Chapter 3, which defines the risks of nitrox diving. From a practical standpoint, most divers will not have a problem with oxygen exposures if they observe normal sport diving limits, avoid decompression or borderline no-decompression situations, and observe reasonable surface intervals.

Using Nitrox

In this course you will learn to dive with nitrox mixtures with various combinations of nitrogen and oxygen, up to a maximum of 40% oxygen. This mixture is more properly referred to as EAN40 (Enriched Air Nitrox 40). You may find that the simplest and most versatile nitrox mixture to use is one with an MOD that works with the sort of dive you regularly do – for example, an EAN32 has an MOD of about 40 metres / 132 feet and therefore is an excellent choice as a "standard" mix for deeper dives within the sport diving limits.

During this course, you will learn how to perform the following:

- Set your dive computer for the proper percentage of oxygen in your mixture.
- Monitor your oxygen exposure while diving using your dive computer.
- Use your computer for planning your initial and repetitive dives (assuming your computer has both of these capabilities).
- Read a nitrox dive table to calculate no-decompression limits for the mixture you are using.

Gas mixtures containing 40% oxygen or less are considered appropriate for "basic" nitrox divers. Gas mixtures containing more than 40% oxygen are sometimes called "advanced nitrox" or "technical nitrox."

Are you ready to start enjoying longer dives with shorter surface intervals?

Let's get started with Computer Nitrox diving!

How to Use this Book

This book will be a reference for you to use during this short course. It is essential for you to read and understand all of the information in this book. If any of the material in this book is unclear to you, please discuss the concepts with your instructor so that you understand all of the information. It is essential for you to understand how to use nitrox effectively, as well as the risks in using nitrox, before you dive with nitrox in open water.

Don't hesitate to take this book with you on your open water diving trips to refresh your understanding of the concepts of nitrox diving between dives. Just be careful, because

divers who don't understand nitrox will probably want to borrow your book and may not want to give it back to you!

Knowledge Quest

At the end of each chapter of this book we will present a series of review questions that your SDI diving instructor will discuss with you. You must understand the concept behind each aspect of using nitrox in order to dive with nitrox correctly.

1. Among the terms divers may use when referring to Nitrox are:

    • _____ Air.

    • Oxygen _____ Air.

    • _____ Air Nitrox.

    • NOAA _____ I and II.

2. The air we normally breathe at sea level contains approximately 79 percent nitrogen and ____ percent oxygen.

3. Nitrox is generally considered to be any mixture of nitrogen and oxygen in which the percentage of oxygen is _____ than that found in air.

4. The term _____ refers to an individual who is qualified to create the Nitrox used to fill scuba cylinders.

5. According to your study materials, among the common Nitrox mixtures sport divers use are:

   - EAN ___ .
   - EAN ___ .
   - EAN ___ .

6. The primary benefits of using Nitrox include longer _____ _____ and shorter _____ _____ .

7. During any 24-hour period, you can be exposed to a Nitrox mixture at its Maximum Operating Depth (MOD) for up to ____ minutes.

chapter two

2

How Nitrox Works to Give You More Bottom Time

In this chapter, you'll learn about:

- What can cause Decompression Sickness and how using Nitrox helps you avoid it
- How using Nitrox can help you extend bottom times
- The concept of Equivalent Air Depth
- What Partial Pressures are and how they relate to Nitrox

To use nitrox effectively, you need to understand the concepts behind the way it works. In this chapter we'll review the concepts behind no-decompression diving, decompression "sickness", and gas mixtures other than air. When you're finished reading this chapter, you should understand how nitrox works to give you longer bottom times and shorter surface intervals.

Understanding Nitrogen and Decompression

As a diver, you know that air contains a mixture of approximately 79% nitrogen and 21% oxygen. At the surface, the nitrogen inside your body is equivalent with the amount of nitrogen in air outside your body. Therefore when you dive and the pressure increases outside your body, your regulator is designed to supply air at a pressure exactly equal to the surrounding pressure. Since the concentration of nitrogen in the air you are breathing is greater than the amount of nitrogen in your body's tissues, your body absorbs more nitrogen at depth. The deeper you dive and the longer you stay underwater, the more nitrogen you will absorb through your lungs into your blood stream. From your blood stream, the nitrogen is carried throughout your body to different tissues.

Wearing a dive computer underwater will calculate approximately the amount of nitrogen absorbed by your body, and indicate when it is time to ascend and the rate at which it is safest to ascend. The dive computer provides a theoretical model of what is happening inside your body, but it does not mirror the exact physiological mechanisms inside your body.

As you return to the surface, and the pressure decreases, this extra nitrogen that you absorbed at depth must be released from your body. If your dive was not too deep or too long, you can make a normal ascent to the surface. However, if your dive lasted for a long time, or you made a deep dive, the dive computer will indicate that you must stop at a particular depth to allow the excess nitrogen in your body time to escape without causing problems. Your computer may require you to make one stop, or a series of stops, commonly known as "decompression stops." During these decompression stops, the excess nitrogen in your body is carried back to the lungs where you exhale it each time you breathe. Smart divers always make a precautionary decompression stop, usually referred to as a "safety stop," for 3-5 minutes at a depth of 3 to 6 metres / 10-20 feet at the end of every dive.

You can also incur a decompression obligation by making repetitive dives over a period of time. While no one dive by itself may exceed the no-decompression limit for a particular depth, nitrogen can accumulate in your body over a series of dives, leading to a decompression obligation for a dive which, by itself, would normally be considered a no-decompression dive.

Decompression diving is not recommended for inexperienced divers. However, if done by those properly trained it can lead to many other exciting dive locations not available in the normal sport diving limits. To properly engage in decompression diving requires specialized training, additional equipment, and topside support. Decompression dives involve more risk than no-decompression dives, and without the proper precautions they become extremely hazardous.

Sport divers should avoid decompression diving by using their dive computers to plan their dives, and carefully monitoring their computers during their dives. However, even if you follow your dive computer's recommendations for dive times and ascent rates and dive within the no-decompression limits, there is always a slight but real risk that you could suffer from decompression sickness (DCS).

It is very important to stay within the no decompression limits the dive computer gives and remain properly hydrated while diving.

Decompression sickness usually occurs when you have an excess amount of nitrogen in your body and you ascend too quickly. The nitrogen comes out of solution and forms a bubble thus disrupting the flow of blood in whatever part of the body it is located. The most common symptoms include, but are not limited to, pain in the joints, numbness, paralysis, loss of balance, muscle weakness, and impaired thinking. First aid for decompression sickness includes treating the diver for shock by laying them down and keeping them either from being too cold or too warm. However, the most important thing to do is provide the diver pure oxygen as soon as possible and transport to a hyperbaric chamber where proper recompression therapy can be performed.

Recompression treatment is extremely expensive and time consuming. The procedure involves placing the diver inside a recompression (hyperbaric) chamber and pressurizing the chamber, usually to a depth of approximately 18 metres / 60 feet. The diver is then brought back to the surface very slowly, during which time there are extended periods where he breathes pure oxygen. Even with prompt, rapid treatment, not all divers who suffer from decompression sickness fully recover. Many are left with permanent disabilities. Thus it is very important to stay within the no decompression limits the dive computer gives and remain properly hydrated while diving.

Using Nitrox to Extend Bottom Time and Avoid Decompression

Many years ago, scientists realized that they could extend the amount of time a diver could work underwater and avoid having to decompress by increasing the amount of oxygen and decreasing the amount of nitrogen in his breathing mixture. Through calculation and experimentation they came up with a series of dive tables used to determine the no-decompression limits for different mixtures of oxygen and nitrogen. This was done in the years before anyone had heard of a dive computer.

For example, a diver using air (21% O2 & 79% N2) who does a dive to 30 metres / 100 feet can only stay there for a maximum of 25 minutes according to US Navy Tables. In contrast, if that same diver were using EAN36 (36% O2 & 64% N2) at the same depth, they could stay 40 minutes. By reducing the amount of nitrogen in the mix the diver in-gases at a slower rate, thus increasing the time he can stay there and avoid decompression.

On the surface, you can breathe gas mixtures containing as little as 16% oxygen and still maintain consciousness. Topside you can also breathe 100% pure oxygen (without any nitrogen), as we already mentioned, which is used in the treatment of decompression sickness.

Underwater, sport, technical, and commercial divers may use different gas mixtures other than normal air. Sport divers use mixtures of nitrox with up to 40% oxygen in the mix. Technical divers, who dive outside of the sport diving limits, may use multiple gas mixtures on a single dive by carrying multiple cylinders, or using special diving gear known as "rebreathers." On deeper dives they may use gas mixtures with less than 16% oxygen for the deep part of their dives and up to 100% oxygen during the decompression phase of their dives.

Commercial divers, who dive to depths in excess of 300 metres / 1000 feet of sea water, use gas mixtures combining helium and oxygen. Helium is used for very deep dives because it has little narcotic effect when compared to nitrogen. For example the gas mixture for an extended dive to 120 metres / 400 feet by a commercial diver might typically be 96% helium and only 4% oxygen!

During World War II, military divers found that they could dive with 100% oxygen, but only use this mixture down to a depth of 6 metres / 20 feet. Below that depth, something about the oxygen caused divers to go into convulsions without warning. This was almost always fatal. Today, we have a better but still incomplete understanding of why oxygen rich breathing mixtures pose problems for divers when used at depth. We've also discovered that divers who use ordinary compressed air to depths in excess of 66 metres / 218 feet of sea water can suffer the same type of convulsions experienced by divers who use pure oxygen to depths in excess of 6 metres / 20 feet. It has been shown mathematically that breathing the oxygen in compressed air at a depth of 66 metres / 218 feet of sea water is roughly the equivalent of breathing pure oxygen at a depth greater than 6 metres / 20 feet of sea water.

While most of the above types of diving would require extended decompression, this information is presented so you can appreciate the complexities that technical divers must face. For sport diving, we limit the range of nitrox mixtures of up to EAN40 that work within the range of sport diving depths. With the proper training and equipment, there are many breathing mixtures that can be used in diving. For the sport diver, nitrox represents the most convenient and economical. As you continue your diver training you may want to learn how to use other breathing mixtures, but nitrox will always be the easiest and most widely available alternative breathing gas to use for sport diving. Talk to your SDI Instructor for more information about other training options.

Equivalent Air Depth

Another concept that you will hear frequently in relation to nitrox is what is known as the "equivalent air depth." Just as we stated above that using pure oxygen at 6 metres / 20 feet of sea water is like using compressed air at 66 metres / 218 feet, we can make similar computations for any depth we choose.

The equivalent air depth is used to compare nitrogen levels for calculating bottom time. In computing the equivalent air depth, what we are really saying is that a dive to a certain number of metres / feet of sea water on nitrox is equivalent to a dive to a depth of a lesser number of metres / feet on air.

In the early days of nitrox diving, when divers used decompression tables, they had to compute the equivalent air depth for every dive they made. With the dive computers that we use today, this is no longer necessary.

The following tables show the equivalent air depths for nitrox mixtures from EAN32 through EAN40.

Metric Example

Look at the column for EAN32 at a depth of 21 metres. If you are breathing EAN32 at 17 metres of sea water (MSW), the decreased amount of nitrogen in the mix will be absorbed by your body as if you were only diving at 17 MSW. With EAN36 at 21 metres of sea water, it is as though you were diving at 16 MSW. Diving with EAN40 to 21 MSW, your body absorbs nitrogen as though you were at 14 MSW. Clearly, the more oxygen there is in the gas mixture you are breathing, the longer you can stay at any given depth without incurring a decompression obligation.

Equivalent Air Depths in Metres

Actual Depth	EAN32	EAN36	EAN40
12	9	8	7
15	12	11	9
18	15	13	12
21	17	16	14
24	20	17	16
27	22	20	19
30	25	23	N/A
33	28	25	N/A
36	30	N/A	N/A
39	33	N/A	N/A

Imperial Example

Look at the column for EAN32 at a depth of 70 feet. If you are breathing EAN32 at 70 feet of sea water (FSW), the decreased amount of nitrogen in the mix will be absorbed by your body as if you were only diving at 56 FSW. With EAN36 at 70 feet of sea water, it is as though you were diving at 50 FSW. Diving with EAN40 to 70 FSW, your body absorbs nitrogen as though you were at 45 FSW. Clearly, the more oxygen there is in the gas mixture you are breathing, the longer you can stay at any given depth without incurring a decompression obligation.

Equivalent Air Depths in Feet

Actual Depth	EAN32	EAN36	EAN40
40	30	26	22
50	38	34	30
60	47	42	38
70	56	50	45
80	64	59	53
90	73	67	60
100	81	75	N/A
110	90	83	N/A
120	99	N/A	N/A
130	107	N/A	N/A

What is the Optimum Nitrox Mixture for Sport Diving?

There is an optimum nitrox mixture for any depth to which sport divers normally dive, down to 40 metres / 132 feet of sea water. That mixture is 68% nitrogen and 32% oxygen (EAN32).

The reason EAN32 is considered the optimum nitrox mixture is because it is the most oxygen rich mixture that you can use right up to the maximum recommended sport diving depth limit of 40 metres / 132 FSW. Gas mixtures that contain a higher percentage of oxygen are not safe at this depth because of a diving problem called Oxygen Toxicity, which will be explained in detail in the next chapter.

The higher the percentage of oxygen used in the mixture, the shallower the "Maximum Operating Depth" or "MOD" is for a particular mixture. As mentioned previously, a nitrox diver can select a particular mixture for his planned depth. The key word here is "planned," because the more oxygen in the mix, the more restricted the maximum operating depth. When you decide to dive with nitrox, you must plan your dive starting at the dive store when your cylinder is filled.

For example, if you dive with a mixture of 62% nitrogen and 38% oxygen – EAN38 – your maximum operating depth must not exceed 32 metres / 105 feet. Since you need to choose your mixture when you have your tank filled at the dive store, selecting EAN38 is restrictive unless you know for a fact you will not be exceeding this depth on your dives.

The maximum operating depth for EAN36 is 34 metres / 113 feet and the maximum operating depth for EAN40 is 30 metres / 99 feet. Note that as the percentage of oxygen in the mixture increases, the maximum operating depth decreases (becomes shallower). When your tank is filled with nitrox, the blender will not always be able to fill your tank with the exact percentage of oxygen that you specify, due to variations in gas temperature, rounding of numbers, and other factors. Therefore it is very important that you must know the exact percentage of oxygen in your tank to adjust your dive computer properly for every dive.

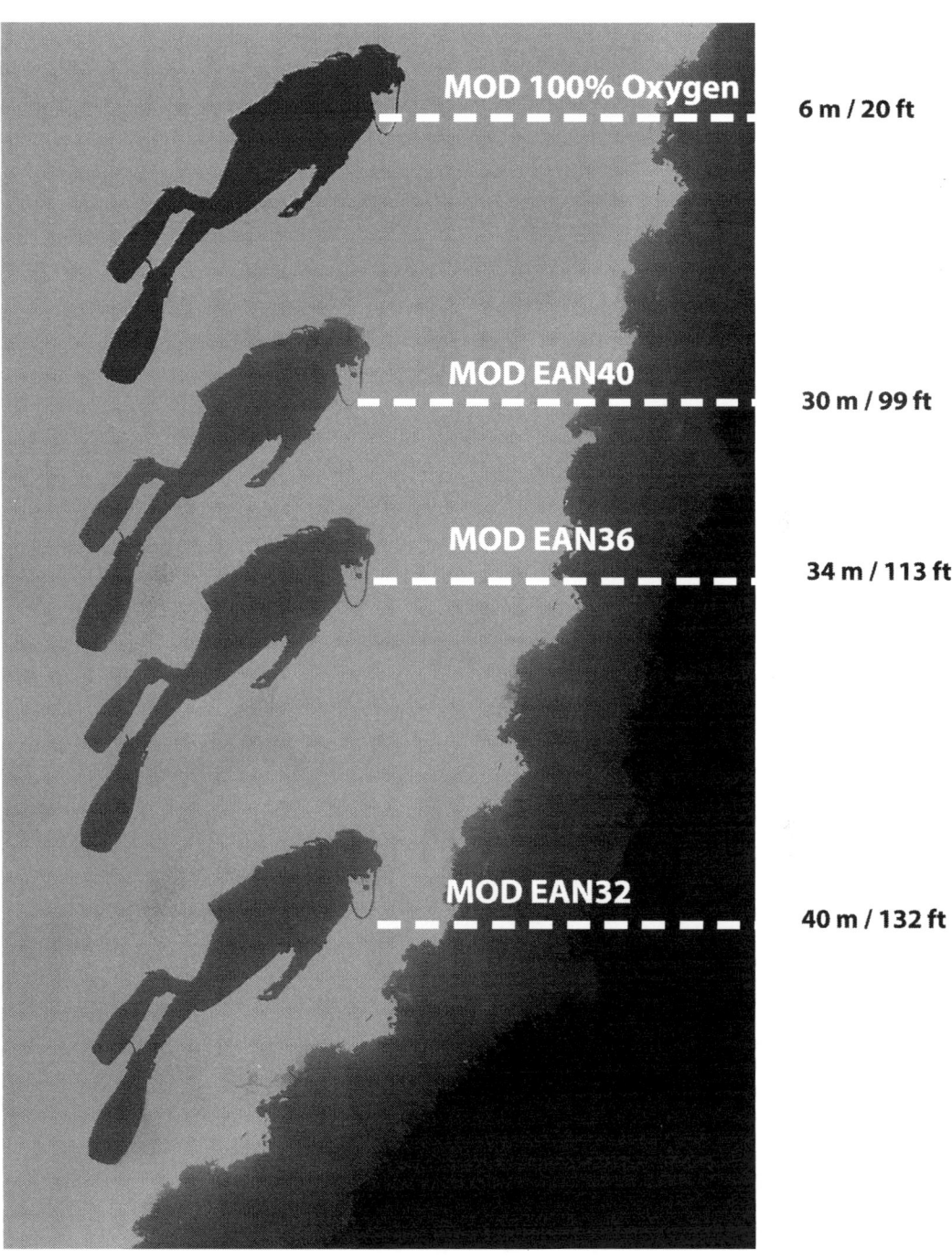

If you look at the Equivalent Air Depth Table (located in the appendix) you will note that the bottom row of the table "stair-steps" upwards, from left to right. The numbers in the bottom row for each gas mixture are the maximum operating depths for each particular nitrox mix.

EAN32 will provide you with a good combination of extended bottom time and unrestricted depth within the sport diving range. In addition, using EAN32 poses less risk in terms of exposure to oxygen than other "richer" mixtures. You'll learn more about the risks of nitrox diving in the next chapter.

Concept of Partial Pressure

There is one more concept that we must understand to use nitrox properly. This is the concept of "partial pressure." It's a simple concept and worth working to understand so that you can execute nitrox dives with a better understanding of what is happening to your body as you breathe higher percentages of oxygen.

In any mixture of two or more gases, such as nitrogen and oxygen, each gas occupies a certain part of the mixture and exerts a certain part of the total pressure exerted by that gas. This portion of the pressure is called, logically enough, its "partial pressure."

The partial pressure of oxygen can be expressed in pounds per square inch or in atmospheres. One atmosphere is equal to the pressure at sea level, or the weight of all of the air above you that presses down on your body. Every 10 metres / 33 feet we descend in the ocean is equal to an additional atmosphere of pressure. At a depth of 10 metres / 33 feet in the ocean we are exposed to two atmospheres of pressure, i.e., the total of the weight of the atmosphere plus the weight of 10 metres / 33 feet of sea water equals two atmospheres.

You will frequently see the partial pressure of oxygen referred to as "ppO2" or more correctly, as "PO2." The "pp" or "P" stands for "partial pressure" and "O2" is the chemical symbol for oxygen. There is nothing magical about this term, and for our purposes all you need to know is that your maximum PO2 must never exceed 1.6. You need to know this information to set and use your nitrox dive computer properly.

For example, on the surface air is made up of approximately 21% O2 and 79% N2. Each exerts a portion of the total pressure to make up air: Oxygen has a partial pressure of .21 and Nitrogen has a partial pressure of .79. As you descend, each of these partial pressures will increase the deeper you go.

Depth		Air		EAN32		EAN36	
m / ft	ATM	ppO$_2$	ppN$_2$	ppO$_2$	ppN$_2$	ppO$_2$	ppN$_2$
0	1	0.21	0.79	0.32	0.68	0.36	0.64
10 / 33	2	0.42	1.58	0.64	1.36	0.72	1.28
20 / 66	3	0.63	2.37	0.96	2.04	1.08	1.92
30 / 99	4	0.84	3.16	1.28	2.72	1.44	2.56
40 /132	5	1.05	3.95	**1.6**	**3.4**	-	-

It is important to note that our bodies can tolerate pure oxygen, or EAN100, at a depth of 6 metres / 20 feet of sea water, which is equal to 1.6 atmospheres; however this type of diving needs additional training as explained earlier in the chapter. For sport diving purposes, we can use EAN32 properly down to 40 metres / 132 feet of sea water, where the pressure of the oxygen in the mixture is equal to 1.6 atmospheres. Breathing pure oxygen at a depth of 6 metres / 20 feet of sea water is the equivalent of breathing EAN32 at 40 metres / 132 feet of sea water in terms of oxygen partial pressure.

Knowledge Quest

Now that you know a bit about gas mixtures other than normal air, discuss these topics with your instructor. You should be able to answer any of the following questions.

Supply the missing words.

1. Dive computers work by calculating the approximate amount of excess nitrogen present in your body, based on factors such as _____ and _____.

2. If you go too deep or stay too long, you may not be able to make a direct ascent to the surface without substantially increasing your risk of _____ _____.

3. A decompression stop involves pausing at a fixed depth for a specified period of _____ to allow excess nitrogen to exit your body more slowly.

4. Decompression diving involves more _____ than no-decompression diving, and without the proper precautions can become extremely _____.

5. Decompression sickness usually occurs when you have an excess amount of _____ _____ in your body and you _____ too quickly.

6. The most common symptoms of decompression sickness can include, but are not limited to, _____ in the joints, _____, paralysis, loss of _____, muscle weakness, and impaired thinking.

7. The *most important* first-aid procedure for a diver suspected of suffering from decompression sickness is administration of pure _____.

8. Once a diver suspected of suffering from decompression has been transported to a medical facility, proper treatment will primarily involve _____ in a hyperbaric chamber.

9. The minimum concentration of oxygen required to maintain consciousness at sea level is ____ percent.

10. The maximum percentage of oxygen that sport divers are likely to use in a Nitrox mixture is ____ percent.

11. The maximum recommended depth for using 100 percent oxygen is _____.

12. The term *EAN32* refers to a Nitrox mixture in which the Fraction of _____ is 32%.

13. The MOD for EAN32 is _____.

14. The term *MOD* stands for _____ _____ Depth.

15. EAN32 is a good choice for Nitrox diving because it provides a good combination of _____ and _____ bottom time.

16. The maximum *partial pressure of oxygen* (PO2) we use in Nitrox diving is _____ .

chapter three

3

Risks Associated with Nitrox Diving

In this chapter, you'll learn about:

- Oxygen Toxicity:
  - What it is
  - How to deal with it
  - How to avoid it

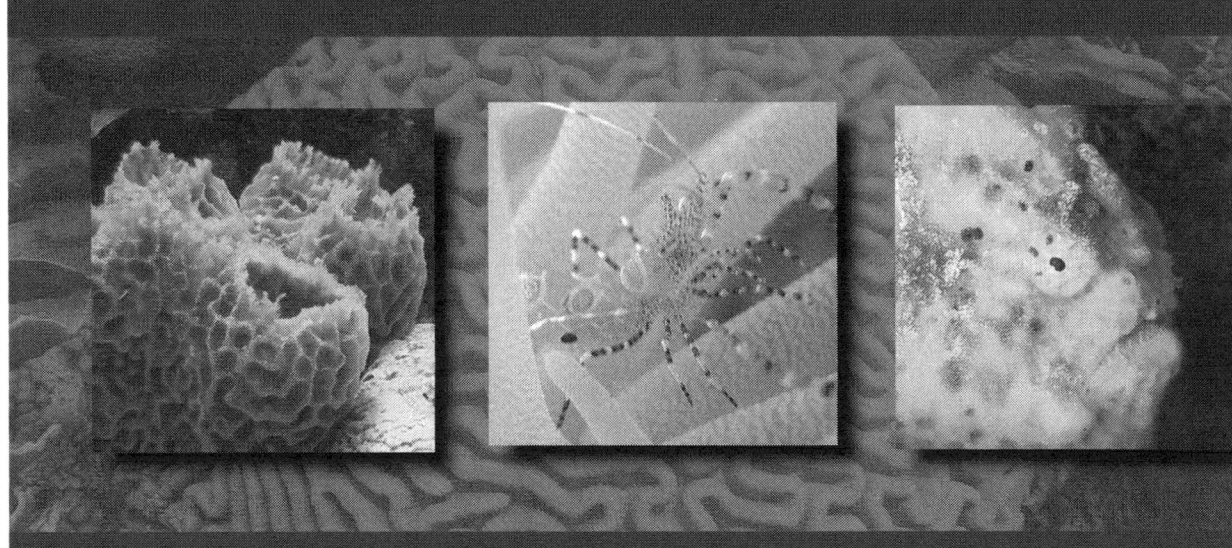

Every type of diving involves some risk because diving is an adventure sport. However, we can minimize the risks through proper instruction, using and maintaining quality diving equipment, staying in good physical condition, and participating in diving on a regular basis.

The risks presented here are not intended to scare you. At Scuba Diving International we believe that you should have a full understanding of all the potential risks in diving. However, these risks can be avoided with proper training, which is what this course is all about. In this chapter you'll learn about these risks, but more importantly you'll learn how to easily avoid them.

Oxygen Toxicity

Oxygen is something we can't live without. Unfortunately, the same element that is essential to our survival can cause us problems underwater. Oxygen toxicity (also referred to as "oxygen poisoning") is a physiological reaction of your body that occurs when you are exposed to breathing mixtures containing high partial pressures of oxygen, or mixtures containing lower partial pressures of oxygen for extended periods. It can be more easily understood as what occurs when the diver breathes a mixture of gas that allows the PO2 to exceed 1.6 by going too deep or exceeding the time limit at a lower PO2. Thus it is the reason you as a diver must set and follow your MOD for every mix on every dive.

Exactly how and why the human body responds in this way is not fully understood, but the effect is like "short circuiting" your nervous system. While oxygen can be toxic to all body tissues, it's most noticeable and immediate effects take place in the lungs and central nervous system. For this reason it is separated into two types of oxygen toxicity.

- **Pulmonary Oxygen toxicity** *can develop when you are exposed to elevated levels of oxygen over long periods of time. However, the length of time involved is well beyond that of most recreational divers. Thus it poses no real risk to sport divers.*
- **Central Nervous System (CNS) Oxygen toxicity** *is of greater concern. This is because all a diver must do is violate the Maximum Operating Depth (MOD) for a particular mix, causing the P02 to rise above 1.6, for the chances of a CNS "hit" increase exponentially.*

When a diver experiences an oxygen "hit," the results can occur without warning, and the consequences can frequently be fatal. The effects of oxygen poisoning are easily remembered by the acronym, "**CONVENTID**." Each one of the letters in this word stands for a specific effect.

CON – stands for convulsions, the most dangerous and potentially fatal risk in using nitrox. The convulsions that occur during oxygen poisoning are similar to an epileptic seizure and may occur without warning. When a convulsion occurs underwater, drowning and death frequently occur. The remaining symptoms may or may not occur prior to a convulsion.

V – The "V" in CONVENTID stands for visual disturbances, which may take the form of "tunnel vision" or the perception of bright flashes of light when nothing is there.

E – The "E" stands for ringing in the ears and other auditory hallucinations.

N – The second "N" stands for nausea. Vomiting underwater is distinctly unpleasant and dangerous.

T – The "T" represents twitching of the muscles, particularly the cheek, nose or eyelids.

I – The "I" indicates irritability or apprehension.

D – The "D" stands for dizziness.

What to do if you or your diving partner experiences a "Hit"

If your diving partner has a convulsion you want to get them to the surface immediately. If you or your partner experience any of the other symptoms of oxygen poisoning, you should immediately ascend to a shallower depth and make a normal ascent to the surface. These other symptoms indicate oxygen poisoning is happening and may occur before a convulsion as a warning. Remember one of the golden rules of diving, "if something seems wrong, it is wrong. Make a safe ascent to the surface immediately".

Fortunately, the effects of oxygen toxicity usually occur when you have violated the maximum depth limit for the mixture you are using. Once you ascend to a shallower depth or exit the water, the symptoms disappear and there appears to be no permanent damage.

The golden rule of diving: "If something seems wrong, it is wrong. Make a safe ascent to the surface immediately".

However, this is not a time to continue your dive; there may be other contributing factors you are unaware of, so it is best to end the dive.

To the best of our knowledge, no one who has used EAN32 and followed the proper procedures for diving with this gas has ever experienced these symptoms. However, if you violate the maximum depth limit of 40 metres / 132 feet, these effects can occur without warning, and the consequences can be disastrous.

Similar to the way in which exposure to increased nitrogen at depth causes your body to absorb more nitrogen, exposures to higher levels of oxygen at depth causes your body to become more sensitive to increased levels of oxygen during subsequent dives. Each dive you make with nitrox during any given 24-hour period increases your oxygen exposure.

Additional Factors that Increase the Risk of "Hit"

There are other factors that can increase the possibility of an "attack" of oxygen poisoning. These factors include the following:

- If you overheat during a dive.
- If you are an insulin dependent diabetic.
- If you suffer from a deficiency of Vitamin E.
- If you have an overactive thyroid (hyperthyroid) gland.
- Diving without proper thermal protection in cold water.
- Taking other drugs that may speed the onset of oxygen toxicity, including adrenocortical hormones, dextroamphetamine, epinephrine, norepinephrine, and paraquat.
- If you are working or swimming hard underwater.
- If you have scar tissue in your lungs you may be more susceptible to oxygen poisoning.

If you suffer from any of the medical problems listed above, or are taking any of the drugs listed above, you must discuss this with your instructor, and you will need medical clearance to dive nitrox from a diving physician. If any of the above conditions apply to you, you must also avoid diving nitrox to its maximum depth limit to reduce your risk.

Preventing Oxygen Toxicity

Oxygen toxicity although it is a very serious type of diving problem, fortunately, avoiding the negative effects of oxygen is easy when using Nitrox. Just follow these precautions and you should never have a problem using nitrox:

- Avoid overheating.

- Wear adequate thermal protection while diving in cold water.

- Never dive with nitrox deeper than the MOD for the mix you are using.

- Avoid heavy exercise while diving with nitrox.

- Get medical clearance for diving if you are an insulin dependent diabetic, and if cleared to dive, restrict your diving to shallower depths.

- Get medical clearance for diving if you are taking any of the other drugs listed in this chapter. If cleared to dive, restrict your diving to shallower depths.

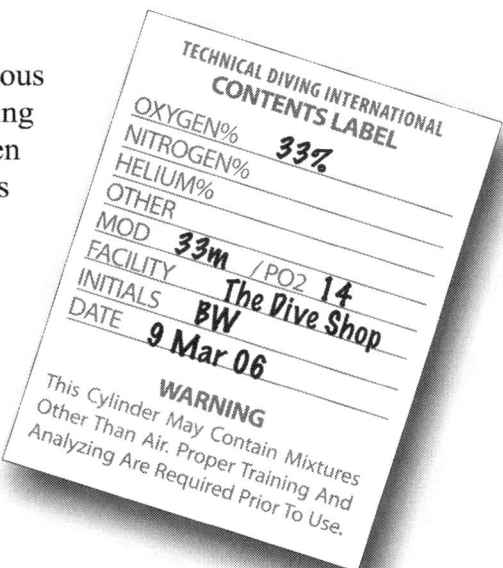

- **ANALYZE** and **LABEL** every cylinder prior to diving.

- Set the appropriate mix in your dive computer and **DO NOT** exceed the limitations it gives you during the dive.

- **NEVER** exceed a **PO2** greater than **1.6**.

Remember that diving to 40 metres / 132 feet of sea water on EAN32 exposes you to the maximum allowable partial pressure of oxygen, or a PO2 of 1.6. Other mixtures have shallower depth limits. If you want to be more conservative, limit your diving to shallower depths or mixes that allow a lower PO2 at the depth you wish to achieve.

Nitrox Repetitive Dive Limitations

Just as we have no-decompression limits in diving due to nitrogen adsorption in our bodies, we have additional limits imposed on us when we use nitrox for diving. If you use nitrogen mixtures that contain high percentages of oxygen, such as EAN40, or above, these limits can become quite restrictive. However, using oxygen mixers lower than EAN40 rarely imposes any additional limits on your diving. We just need to be aware of them and monitor for them.

For your dive computer to work properly, it must be set for the mixture you are using before you enter the water.

There are various terms that are used to denote your exposure to higher levels of oxygen while diving with nitrox. You may hear people talk about CNS (Central Nervous System) oxygen limits, OTUs (Oxygen Tolerance Units), OLF (Oxygen Limit Fraction), OTLs (Oxygen Time Limits), or use other terminology. At Scuba Diving International we prefer to use the term Oxygen Time Limit when we are referring to the maximum exposure you can have to enriched oxygen mixtures underwater. However, your nitrox dive computer may use slightly different terminology. It is important for you to understand how your computer measures oxygen exposure and provides warnings for this aspect of your dives.

Nitrox dive computers are designed to compute oxygen exposures, no-decompression limits, and repetitive dive information for the specific gas mixture you are using. For your computer to work properly, it must be set for the mixture you are using before you enter the water. You will learn more about this in the chapters on equipment selection, dive planning, and making nitrox dives. If you are using an air diving computer, rather than a nitrox computer, you will be limited by the no-decompression limits of your computer to such an extent that oxygen exposure will not be a problem.

Almost all modern dive computers provide alarms that will warn you when you are reaching the limits of oxygen exposure for the time, depth and mixture you are using. Some will also be set to activate an alarm when you reach the maximum PO2 for the mixture in your tank. These alarms may be both visual and audible. Some computers also compare decompression time, oxygen exposure, and air consumption and provide warnings about which of these factors will most immediately affect your dive.

Note that most dive computers provide single dive times that are much shorter, but have the capability to compute a multi-level dive, taking into account time spent at progressively shallower depths. Consequently, the time permitted by a dive computer on a single, non-repetitive dive is usually longer than what a table would allow, provided that you do not spend your entire time at the maximum depth of the dive. Nitrox dive computers, and dive computers in general, are a much more convenient, and usually more accurate way to compute depth and time especially when you are making repetitive dives within a 24 hour period.

Chapter 3 | Risks Associated with Nitrox Diving

Recommended Surface Intervals for Nitrox Divers

The minimum recommended surface interval for divers using nitrox is 30 minutes, although a 60-minute interval is preferred. After long dives/extended exposures, a two-hour (120-minute) surface interval is recommended. The reason for this is based on breathing higher than normal PO2 means your body needs a period of time to compensate for that exposure. A 60 minute surface interval definitely reduces the risk of having an Oxygen "hit" when conducting multiple dives.

PO2	Single Limit Dive Time in Minutes	24 Hour Limit Time in Minutes
0.6	720	720
0.7	540	540
0.8	450	450
0.9	360	360
1.0	300	300
1.1	240	270
1.2	210	240
1.3	180	210
1.4	150	180
1.5	120	180
1.6	45	150

NOAA Oxygen Exposure Limits for Working Divers

Knowledge Quest

1. Oxygen toxicity is a physiological reaction of your body that occurs when you are exposed to breathing mixtures containing _____ partial pressures of oxygen, or mixtures containing _____ partial pressures of oxygen for extended periods.

2. The primary risk associated with Nitrox diving (as opposed to diving air) is _____ toxicity or poisoning.

3. List the words represented by the acronym *CONVENTID*.

4. The following are factors that may increase a diver's susceptibility to oxygen toxicity:

   - Over _____.
   - _____-dependent diabetes.
   - Vitamin ___ deficiency.
   - An _____ thyroid (hyperthyroid) gland.
   - Inadequate _____ protection.
   - Use of _____ hormones, dextroamphetamine, _____, norepinephrine, and/or paraquat.
   - Scar tissue in the _____.

5. The following are things divers can do to help minimize the general risks associated with Nitrox and other forms of diving:

   - Get the _____ necessary for the type of diving you are doing.
   - Use only complete and well-maintained _____.
   - Maintain adequate health and _____ for diving.
   - _____ regularly.

6. Additional steps Nitrox divers can take to help avoid oxygen toxicity include:

   - Analyze and _____ every Nitrox cylinder.
   - Never exceed your mixture's _____.
   - Always program your dive computer for the _____ of the gas mixture you are using.
   - Never exceed a PO2 of ____.

7. What are the two gases that a Nitrox diving computer takes into consideration when computing your allowable bottom time?

8. The recommended surface interval after extended dives with Nitrox is ____ minutes.

chapter four

Selecting Equipment for Nitrox Diving

In this chapter, you'll learn about:

- Nitrox compatible diving equipment and its preparation

- How to properly label a cylinder

- Nitrox dive computers

- Equipment risks associated with oxygen

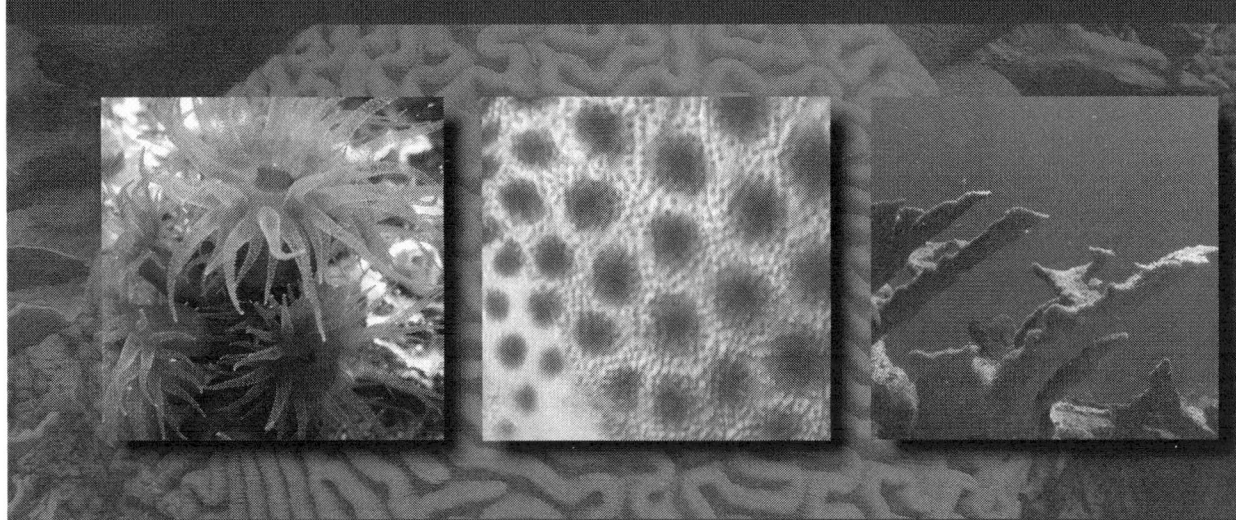

If you already own your own dive gear – exposure suit, BCD, regulators and so on – you can dive with nitrox mixtures containing 40% oxygen or less without purchasing any additional equipment. There are a couple of things you may contemplate purchasing (a simple nitrox analyzer for example), but you can take full advantage of diving nitrox without any further financial outlay.

That said, we will take a look at some minor gear modifications that you'll need to make to your gear; and let's also take note of a couple of things that you should know in case you decide to purchase dedicated nitrox diving gear some time in the future.

Tank Preparation, Marking and Identification

If you own tanks and intend to use them for nitrox diving (and you should!) there are a couple of things you need to do before filling them with your personal mix.

The Blending Method Counts: SDI dive centers, resorts and liveaboards employ a variety of methods to create Nitrox, including partial-pressure blending in dive cylinders and storage bottles, continuous-blending systems and separation membranes (see Appendix I for a brief description of each of these methods).

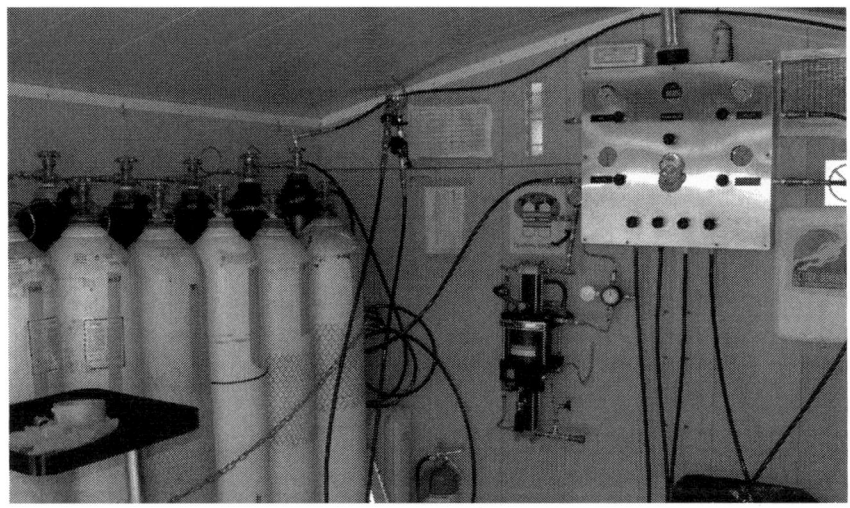

Sport divers don't need to understand the particulars of most of these methods. They do need to be aware, however, that the first of these methods — partial pressure blending in the end users' cylinders — exposes both cylinders and valves to oxygen concentrations in excess of 40 percent, at pressures far greater than regulator intermediate pressure. Thus, these cylinders and valves must be oxygen clean and oxygen service rated, to reduce the risk of fire or explosion.

Whether or not to O2 clean other equipment items is dictated by a hierarchy of practices.

- Local laws, regulations and standards of practice always take precedence over any less-strict requirements.

- Manufacturer's specifications also take precedence over any less-strict requirements, as dive operators cannot defend a decision based on the fact they presume to "know better" than the engineers who designed a particular piece of equipment.

- Absent the precedence of either of these two factors, the standard of practice is to apply what is known as the 40 Percent Rule.

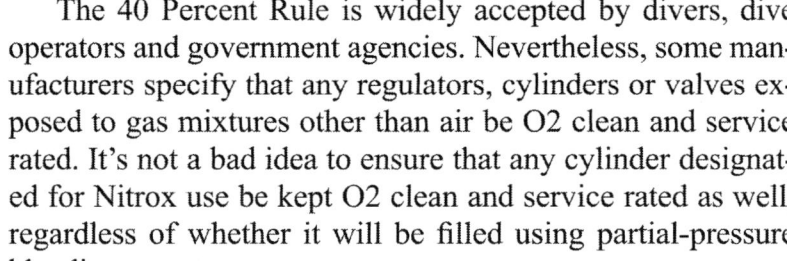

The 40 Percent Rule

The essence of the 40 Percent Rule is that, barring the conditions outlined above, if a regulator, cylinder or valve will not be exposed to gas mixtures with an FO2 greater than 40 percent, at pressures greater than regulator intermediate pressure, they need not be O2 clean or service rated.

The 40 Percent Rule is widely accepted by divers, dive operators and government agencies. Nevertheless, some manufacturers specify that any regulators, cylinders or valves exposed to gas mixtures other than air be O2 clean and service rated. It's not a bad idea to ensure that any cylinder designated for Nitrox use be kept O2 clean and service rated as well, regardless of whether it will be filled using partial-pressure blending or not.

Oxygen Compatible Air

It is important to understand that it is not merely sufficient to have those equipment items that require it O2 cleaned and prepared for Nitrox use. You must also maintain the O2 service rating by exposing these items only to gas mixtures created using oxygen-compatible air.

- **Standard Scuba Air** — although very clean and dry — still contains trace amounts of hydrocarbons and other contaminants. If allowed to collect on the internal surfaces of cylinders, regulators and valves, these create a risk of fire and/or explosion — a risk that O2 cleaning will eliminate.

- **Oxygen-Compatible Air**, on the other hand, is virtually free of hydrocarbons and contaminants. By making certain that the internal surfaces of cylinders, regulators and valves only come in contact with oxygen-compatible air, or gas mixtures created using oxygen-compatible air, you effectively eliminate the risk of fire or explosion, and maintain your equipment's O2 service rating.

It is impossible for a dive operator to determine, simply by looking at cylinder markings that indicate the cylinder was O2 cleaned within the past year, that a cylinder and valve have not been exposed to air or gas mixtures that would invalidate its O2 service rating. Thus, it is the responsibility of the divers who own or use this equipment to:

- Only allow this equipment to come in contact with oxygen-compatible air or gas mixtures, or...

- If the equipment does come in contact with standard scuba air, to remove any markings that indicate it is O2 clean, and not represent to dive operators that any such cylinders are suitable to be filled with Nitrox through in-cylinder partial-pressure blending.

If your cylinder is O_2 service rated, you must use only oxygen compatible air.

Chapter 4 | Selecting Equipment for Nitrox Diving

Nitrox divers often have their cylinders refilled with air for dives in which having Nitrox may not offer any appreciable benefit. If you do so, and if your cylinder is O2 service rated, you must use only oxygen compatible air.

Tank Marking and Identification

Any time you fill a tank with nitrox it must be identified as such. This will help to prevent accidents in the event that someone uses a tank filled with nitrox without taking the proper precautions. The industry standard for tanks filled with nitrox is to mark the tank with both a "tank wrap," as well as to identify the mixture with a label or tag.

A nitrox tank wrap is a sticky backed tape, usually four or five inches wide, that is designed to completely encircle the diameter of the tank. The tape is usually printed in yellow with bold green letters with the word "NITROX" printed continuously on it. This tape makes it quick and easy to spot a nitrox bottle in a group of tanks.

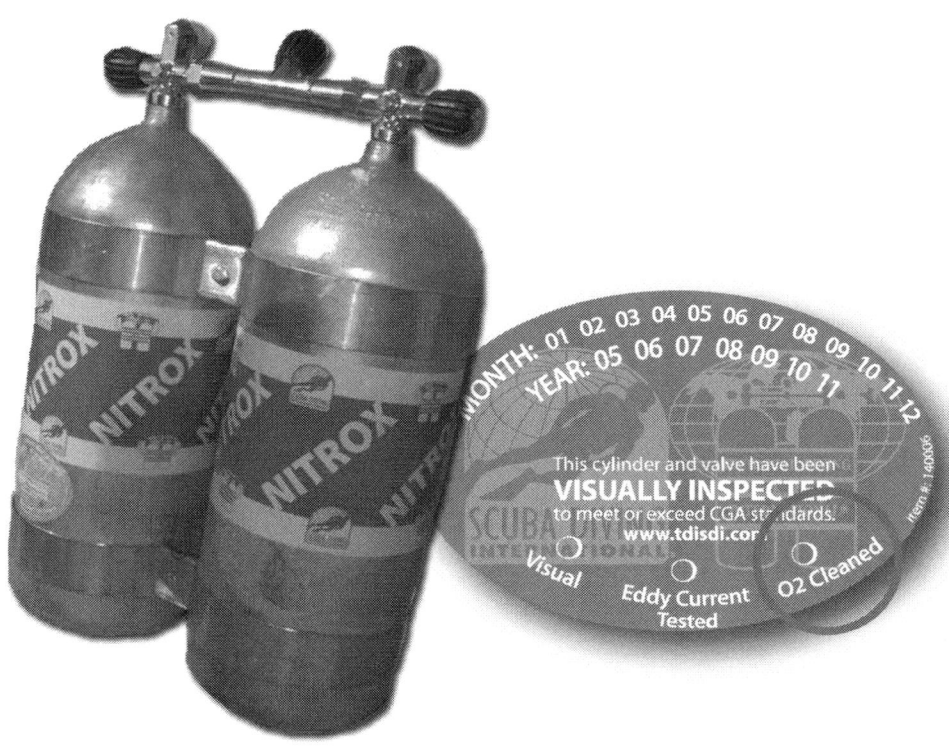

It is important to note that although the industry standard is described and pictured here, some countries require different looking labels by law. Consult a local SDI dive center to find out what the local laws require prior to diving.

Any tank used for nitrox diving must also have a tag or label attached to it indicating the exact nitrox mixture used in the tank and its MOD. Some shops use plastic tags that can be written on and reused, some use labels stuck to the tank itself, others use duct tape stuck to the cylinder neck. It doesn't matter which style of marking device is used as long as the information is instantly available on the tank.

Regulators Designed for Nitrox Service

As we've already mentioned, it is not essential to buy a special regulator if you only plan to dive with mixtures containing 40% oxygen or less. Almost any regulator you already own can be used for this type of service with no special modifications or cleaning, although some manufacturers may void a warranty when a regulator not designed for nitrox service is used with nitrox. Check with your instructor or dive center before you start to use an existing regulator with enriched air mixtures.

Many diving equipment manufacturers now sell regulators specifically designed for nitrox service. These regulators can usually be identified by yellow and/or green rings on the first stage and by yellow and/or green second stages. But the real difference is more than skin deep, and nitrox regulators have special o-rings, nitrox compatible seats, and use special lubricants. The real value of a dedicated nitrox regulator is in situations where levels of oxygen higher than 40% will be used.

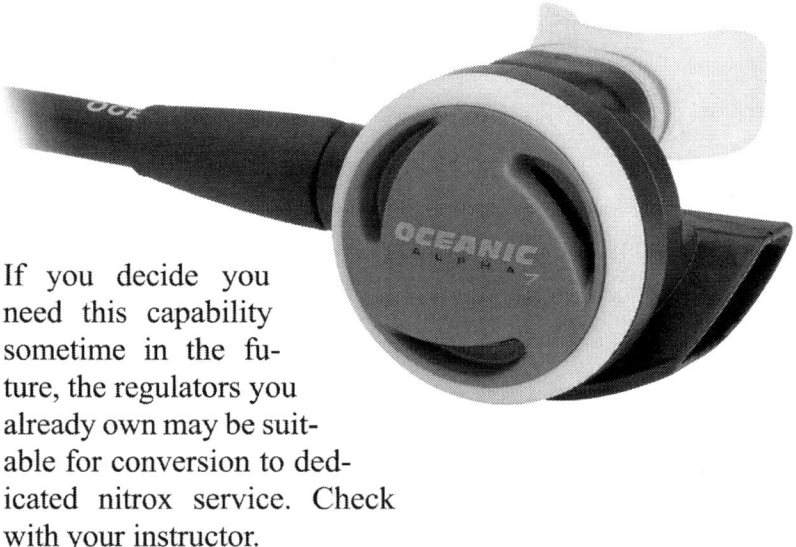

If you decide you need this capability sometime in the future, the regulators you already own may be suitable for conversion to dedicated nitrox service. Check with your instructor.

In addition to the markings that are used on regulators specifically designed for nitrox service, you may also want to purchase a colored plastic hose wrap, designed to cover the low pressure hose connecting the first and second stages of your regulator. This is an additional method of identifying a regulator that will be used especially for nitrox service.

Remember that if you purchase a regulator specifically for nitrox you must not use it with any cylinders that have not been cleaned for oxygen service and filled at an oxygen safe facility. Use with anything but oxygen safe gas mixtures may expose the regulator to oils and contaminants that can lead to an oxygen fire or explosion. An oxygen fire could be fatal to you or anyone close by you.

Nitrox Dive Computers

A prerequisite for this course is that you will be using a programmable nitrox computer. Almost every manufacturer today offers nitrox dive computers at prices that put them well within the budget of the majority of active divers. You may also find that many SDI Dive Centers and resorts rent nitrox programmable computers.

Renting a nitrox computer may be an excellent way to check out a specific model before buying, but be careful that you fully understand how your rented computer works before diving it. If you rent a computer from a dive center, be sure to ask them to provide you with a copy of the manual, or at the very least, have them explain the computer's functions to you so that you fully understand them.

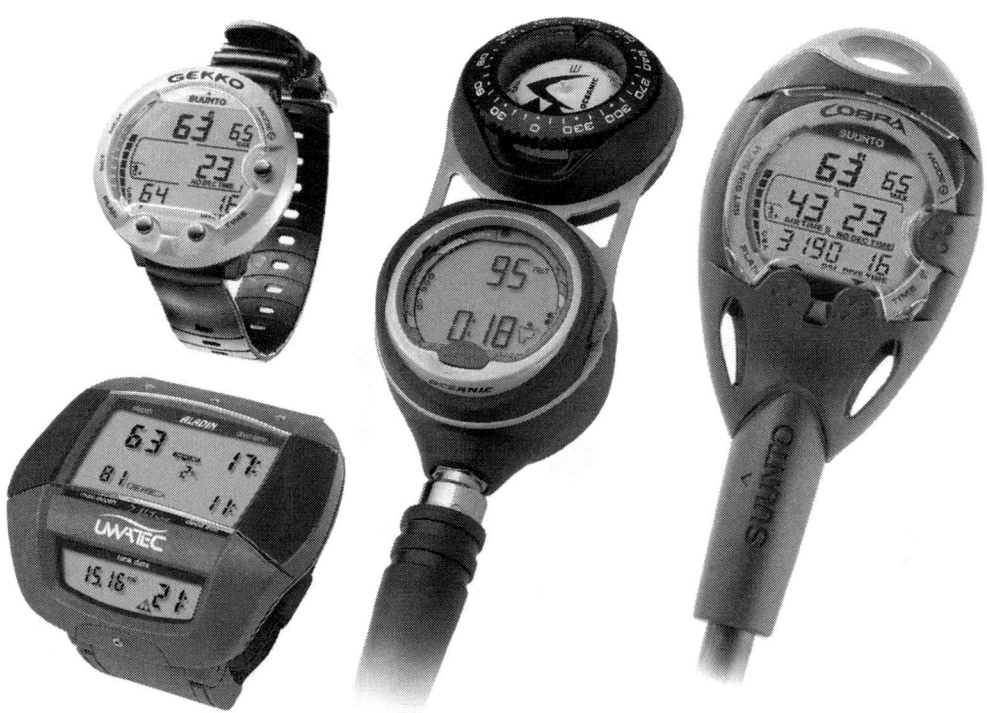

Most dedicated nitrox computers simultaneously track and display your nitrogen absorption for decompression calculations and your oxygen exposure. If you are making multiple deep dives in a single day, this type of information is extremely important.

Some of the more sophisticated models even allow you to change gas mixtures while diving, a technique used by many technical divers who switch to mixtures containing higher percentages of oxygen for decompression.

Most modern nitrox dive computers allow you to set the percentage of oxygen in your breathing mix anywhere between 21% and 50% oxygen. A few will even allow richer mixtures. However, most require that the percentage of oxygen in the mixture be set before you enter the water. This procedure must be done prior to the start of every dive.

Some nitrox dive computers will default to 21% oxygen (air) when they are first "booted up" at the start of a dive day. Others will retain whatever mixture at which you set them. Whatever type of computer you use, it is essential that you verify that your computer is properly set for the mixture you will be using before each dive. This is essential for the computer to calculate your decompression and oxygen exposure properly.

In most other ways, nitrox dive computers do not differ from air diving computers. They provide the same type of dive planning, repetitive dive calculations, and log functions.

In addition to programming your computer with the information on the mixture you will be using, you will also need to program it with the maximum partial pressure to which you are willing to expose yourself. To get the maximum depth capability from EAN32 you need to program your computer for a partial pressure of oxygen of 1.6. If you want to be more conservative, you can set your dive computer for a PO_2 of 1.5 or 1.4.

> *It is essential that you verify that your computer is properly set for the mixture you will be using before each dive.*

It's important to remember that none of the dive computers currently available provide an exact measurement of the nitrogen and oxygen levels inside your body. The computer only provides a mathematical model of what diving physiologists think is going on. Even if you follow your dive computer exactly, it's still possible to experience decompression sickness or oxygen toxicity. However, these same risks apply to using dive tables, with the added risk that it is far more likely that a diver will make mistakes in his calculations when using tables and formulas.

You may also see divers using air diving computers with nitrox. This is far from an ideal situation because not only does one lose the advantage of the additional bottom time provided by using enriched air, air computers do not track one's exposure to oxygen and this must be done manually.

Thermal Protection is Needed for Longer Dives

To get the full benefit of diving with nitrox, you'll need to be sure that you are wearing adequate thermal protection for the waters where you dive. Whether you dive in the tropics or in colder waters, the extended bottom times provided by nitrox will usually necessitate more thermal protection/insulation than you might ordinarily wear.

While you might be able to dive in the Caribbean wearing a dive skin for short duration dives, when using nitrox you may need to switch to wearing a tropical shorty wetsuit. The fact is that the more diving you do, the more likely it is that you'll get cold, even in warmer waters.

To reap the maximum benefits of nitrox in waters colder than about 18 degrees Celsius / about 65 degrees Fahrenheit, you should consider a dry suit for optimal thermal protection. Dry suits are not difficult to use, but they do require additional training so ask your instructor about drysuit diving.

Oxygen Analyzer

Oxygen analyzers are electronic devices that are used to measure the percentage of oxygen in a gas mixture. They run on batteries and most are equipped with a "fuel cell" designed to record the percentage of oxygen in a gas mixture. Most modern oxygen analyzers have a digital display that shows the reading. All dive centers that fill nitrox cylinders have oxygen analyzers. They use them to check each cylinder after it has been filled to be sure that it contains the correct mixture of nitrogen and oxygen.

Oxygen analyzers are simple devices to use. Your instructor will show you how to use one during this course. In most cases, they require nothing more than to be turned on and allowed to stabilize while reading room air. After the analyzer has been on for a few minutes, it should read very close to 21% oxygen. If it does not, it is a simple matter to calibrate the analyzer to the correct reading, usually by turning a dial located on the front of the unit.

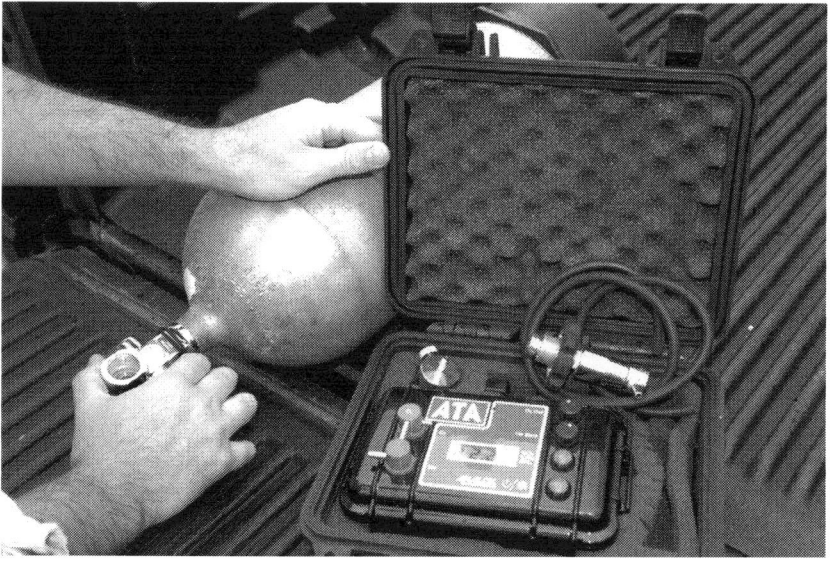

Once the analyzer has been calibrated, it is connected to your cylinder using some type of device that will restrict the flow of nitrox to the analyzer so it is not exposed to high pressure. Once the nitrox is flowing steadily to the analyzer and the reading has stabilized, the reading is noted.

It isn't necessary to purchase your own oxygen analyzer, although most serious nitrox divers end up purchasing their own units for use at home or on dive trips. An analyzer is especially useful for technical divers who own more than one nitrox cylinder and have them filled with different mixtures. In the event a tag is lost or falls off, it is a simple matter to re-analyze your own cylinder. You must always know what gas mixture is in your cylinder.

You must always know what gas mixture is in your cylinder.

Equipment That Doesn't Need to be Oxygen Clean

Equipment that is exposed to low pressure oxygen, such as buoyancy compensators and their low pressure inflators and dry suit inflation valves do not need to be cleaned or lubricated for oxygen service. There is very little chance of explosion or fire danger with dive gear that is exposed to low pressure oxygen.

Fire and Explosion Risks: A final word about nitrox safety

In your research into Nitrox, you may have heard that there are fire and explosion risks when you use gas mixtures that have oxygen levels greater than present in air (higher than 21%).

Certainly, gas mixtures containing 41% or more oxygen are susceptible to fire and explosion if improperly handled. When high-pressure oxygen comes into contact with hydrocarbons, such as oil, the potential for fire and explosion is very real. Oxygen fueled fires are swift to spread, usually difficult to extinguish and often result in tragic loss of property and sometimes lives.

However, the mixtures you will encounter as an SDI nitrox diver will contain 40% or less oxygen and are not considered at risk. That said, some diving equipment manufacturers insist that your equipment must be specially cleaned for oxygen service and use oxygen compatible seals and components if it is used for anything but air. If you buy this type of equipment you must comply with the manufacturer's conditions or the warranty on your equipment may be void.

Oxygen cleaning must be performed by a trained technician in a clean environment, using cleaning agents and replacement components that have been deemed "safe" for this application.

If your gear is designed for oxygen service, such as a tank or regulator, and is used with systems that are not "oxygen clean," the gear must be considered "contaminated" and may not used with nitrox mixtures until it has been cleaned again. For this reason, if you loan your nitrox compatible diving gear to another nitrox diver, you must be sure that they understand that they can only use it with gases and systems that are oxygen clean.

Knowledge Quest

Are you ready to pick out your nitrox diving computer? Do you need a dedicated nitrox regulator? Discuss these issues with your instructor.

1. A large, tank-encircling, green and yellow decal with the words *Enriched Air* and/or _____ on it is frequently referred to as a *tank wrap*.

2. The two most important pieces of information that will appear on a Nitrox fill tag or label are _____ and _____.

3. Regulators that will be exposed to oxygen concentrations of less than ___ percent need no special preparation unless required by _____ specifications or local laws/regulations.

4. The most important setting that must be made to your Nitrox computer before every dive is the _____ of your breathing mixture.

5. To compensate for _____ loss on longer dives, you may need additional _____ protection for Nitrox diving.

6. An _____ _____ is an electronic device used to measure the percentage of oxygen in a gas mixture.

chapter five
5

Filling Your Cylinders with Nitrox -
Getting ready for your Nitrox dives

In this chapter, you'll learn about:

- What nitrox mixture is the right one for the dive you plan

- How a nitrox cylinder is filled

- Nitrox dive computers

- How to analyze the nitrox mixture in the cylinder

Of course the only way to actually dive with nitrox, is to have your cylinders filled at a qualified dive center. Although this process is very similar to filling an air cylinder, there are a few differences you need to take into consideration.

Selecting Your Mixture

Making the correct choice depends entirely on two issues: Since each "flavor" of nitrox has a different MOD, you need to make sure yours is safe at your maximum depth. And what partial pressure of oxygen is right for your conditions. Many experienced nitrox divers use a PO2 of 1.6 in warm, calm water but back the PO2 to 1.4 in colder more challenging conditions. Great aids in dive planning are the Nitrox MOD tables.

Chapter 5 | Filling Your Cylinders with Nitrox

Metric Example

For example, the maximum depth we are going to dive is 35 metres and do not want to exceed a PO2 of 1.4. Locate the box in the table below with both of those values in it. If you do not find your depth, simply round to the next deepest depth. Then move vertically up to the find the EAN mix best for this dive, EAN30. It's that simple. By moving horizontally from your initial starting point you will also notice this dive will have an EAD of 30 metres.

ACTUAL DEPTH
PO2 with current mix at current depth

Just remember, find the MOD of your mix and go no deeper!

Equivalent Air Depths, Partial Pressures of Oxygen and Maximum Operating Depths

EAD	FO₂	21%	22%	23%	24%	25%	26%	27%	28%	29%	30%	31%	32%	33%	34%	35%	36%	37%	38%	39%	40%
9		9 / 0.4	9 / 0.5	9 / 0.5	9 / 0.5	10 / 0.5	10 / 0.6	10 / 0.6	10 / 0.7	11 / 0.7	11 / 0.7	12 / 0.8	12 / 0.8	12 / 0.8	13 / 0.9	13 / 0.9	13 / 0.9	14 / 1.0	14 / 1.0	15 / 1.0
12		12 / 0.5	12 / 0.5	12 / 0.6	12 / 0.6	13 / 0.6	13 / 0.6	13 / 0.7	14 / 0.7	14 / 0.7	15 / 0.8	15 / 0.8	15 / 0.9	16 / 0.9	16 / 1.0	17 / 1.0	17 / 1.0	18 / 1.1	18 / 1.1	18 / 1.2
15		15 / 0.6	15 / 0.6	15 / 0.6	15 / 0.6	16 / 0.7	16 / 0.7	17 / 0.8	17 / 0.8	17 / 0.8	18 / 0.9	18 / 1.0	19 / 1.0	19 / 1.0	20 / 1.1	20 / 1.1	21 / 1.2	21 / 1.2	22 / 1.3	22 / 1.3
18		18 / 0.6	18 / 0.7	18 / 0.7	19 / 0.8	19 / 0.8	19 / 0.9	20 / 0.9	20 / 0.9	21 / 1.0	22 / 1.0	22 / 1.1	23 / 1.1	23 / 1.2	24 / 1.2	24 / 1.3	25 / 1.3	25 / 1.4	26 / 1.5	26 / 1.5
21		21 / 0.7	21 / 0.7	21 / 0.8	22 / 0.8	22 / 0.8	23 / 0.9	23 / 0.9	24 / 1.0	24 / 1.0	25 / 1.1	26 / 1.2	26 / 1.2	27 / 1.3	27 / 1.3	28 / 1.4	28 / 1.5	29 / 1.5	30 / 1.6	30 / 1.6
24		24 / 0.8	24 / 0.8	24 / 0.8	25 / 0.9	25 / 0.9	26 / 1.0	27 / 1.0	27 / 1.1	28 / 1.1	28 / 1.2	29 / 1.3	30 / 1.3	30 / 1.4	31 / 1.5	31 / 1.5	32 / 1.6	33 / 1.7	34 / 1.8	34 / 1.8
27		27 / 0.8	27 / 0.9	27 / 1.0	28 / 1.0	28 / 1.0	29 / 1.1	30 / 1.1	30 / 1.2	31 / 1.2	31 / 1.3	32 / 1.4	32 / 1.4	33 / 1.5	34 / 1.5	34 / 1.6	35 / 1.7	36 / 1.8		
30		30 / 0.9	31 / 1.0	31 / 1.0	32 / 1.1	32 / 1.1	33 / 1.2	34 / 1.3	35 / 1.3	35 / 1.4	35 / 1.4	36 / 1.5	37 / 1.6	37 / 1.6	38 / 1.7					
33		33 / 1.0	33 / 1.0	34 / 1.1	34 / 1.1	35 / 1.2	35 / 1.2	36 / 1.3	37 / 1.4	37 / 1.4	38 / 1.5	39 / 1.6	39 / 1.6	40 / 1.7	41 / 1.8					
36		36 / 1.0	36 / 1.1	37 / 1.1	37 / 1.2	38 / 1.2	39 / 1.3	39 / 1.4	40 / 1.4	41 / 1.5	41 / 1.6	42 / 1.7	43 / 1.7							
39		39 / 1.1	39 / 1.1	40 / 1.2	40 / 1.3	41 / 1.4	42 / 1.4	43 / 1.5	43 / 1.5	44 / 1.6	45 / 1.7									
42		42 / 1.1	42 / 1.2	43 / 1.3	44 / 1.3	44 / 1.4	45 / 1.5	46 / 1.6	47 / 1.6	47 / 1.7										

Maximum Operating Depths

PO₂																					
1.4		56	53	50	48	46	43	41	40	38	36	35	33	32	31	30	28	27	26	25	25
1.5		61	58	55	52	50	47	45	43	41	40	38	36	35	34	32	31	30	29	28	27
1.6		66	62	59	56	54	51	49	47	45	43	41	40	38	37	35	34	33	32	31	30

WARNING
Susceptibility to decompression sickness and oxygen toxicity can vary from person to person, and from day to day • No dive table, computer or planning device can guarantee that — even if used correctly — you will not suffer from one or both of these problems • therefore, the user must assume all risks associated with the use of this product • Caution is recommended

Instructions for Use
- To determine Equivalent Air Depth (EAD) and partial pressure of oxygen (PO2), start at the FO2 value for the mixture used.
- Move down the FO2 column until you find the depth value that exactly equals or just exceeds the actual dive depth.
- The PO2 for this depth will appear immediately below this number.
- To determine the EAD, move left from the actual depth value to find the Equivalent Air Depth in the far left-hand column.
- As long as the actual dive depth does not exceed the Maximum Operating Depth (MOD) shown at the bottom of the table, it is okay to use the PO2 associated with that MOD.
- Depths shown are in Meters of salt water at sea level.
- Fractional depth values have been rounded down to the next shallower integer. Fractional PO2 values are have been rounded upward to the next higher 0.1

© 2006, SDI/TDI/ERDI • EAD_Metric_v0517

Imperial Example

For example, the maximum depth we are going to dive is 117 feet and do not want to exceed a PO2 of 1.4. Locate the box in the table below with both of those values in it. If you do not find your depth, simply round to the next deepest depth. Then move vertically up to the find the EAN mix best for this dive, EAN30. It's that simple. By moving horizontally from your initial starting point you will also notice this dive will have an EAD of 100 feet.

ACTUAL DEPTH — 117
PO2 with current mix at current depth — 1.4

Just remember, find the MOD of your mix and go no deeper!

Equivalent Air Depths, Partial Pressures of Oxygen and Maximum Operating Depths

EAD	FO₂	21%	22%	23%	24%	25%	26%	27%	28%	29%	30%	31%	32%	33%	34%	35%	36%	37%	38%	39%	40%
30		30 / 0.4	30 / 0.5	31 / 0.5	32 / 0.5	33 / 0.5	34 / 0.6	35 / 0.6	36 / 0.6	37 / 0.7	38 / 0.7	39 / 0.7	40 / 0.8	41 / 0.8	42 / 0.8	43 / 0.9	44 / 0.9	46 / 0.9	47 / 1.0	48 / 1.0	49 / 1.0
40		40 / 0.5	40 / 0.5	41 / 0.6	42 / 0.6	43 / 0.6	44 / 0.7	46 / 0.7	47 / 0.7	48 / 0.8	49 / 0.8	50 / 0.8	51 / 0.9	53 / 0.9	54 / 0.9	55 / 1.0	57 / 1.0	58 / 1.1	60 / 1.1	61 / 1.2	63 / 1.2
50		50 / 0.6	51 / 0.6	52 / 0.6	53 / 0.7	54 / 0.7	55 / 0.7	56 / 0.8	58 / 0.8	59 / 0.9	60 / 0.9	62 / 0.9	63 / 1.0	64 / 1.0	66 / 1.1	67 / 1.1	69 / 1.2	71 / 1.2	72 / 1.3	74 / 1.3	76 / 1.4
60		60 / 0.6	61 / 0.7	62 / 0.7	63 / 0.7	64 / 0.8	66 / 0.8	67 / 0.9	69 / 0.9	70 / 0.9	71 / 1.0	73 / 1.0	75 / 1.1	76 / 1.1	78 / 1.2	80 / 1.2	81 / 1.3	83 / 1.4	85 / 1.4	87 / 1.5	89 / 1.5
70		70 / 0.7	71 / 0.7	72 / 0.8	74 / 0.8	75 / 0.9	76 / 0.9	78 / 1.0	80 / 1.0	81 / 1.1	83 / 1.1	84 / 1.1	86 / 1.2	88 / 1.3	90 / 1.3	92 / 1.4	94 / 1.4	96 / 1.5	98 / 1.6	100 / 1.6	102 / 1.6
80		80 / 0.8	81 / 0.8	82 / 0.9	84 / 0.9	86 / 0.9	87 / 1.0	89 / 1.0	91 / 1.1	92 / 1.1	94 / 1.2	96 / 1.3	98 / 1.3	100 / 1.4	102 / 1.4	104 / 1.5	106 / 1.6	108 / 1.6	110 / 1.7	113 / 1.8	
90		90 / 0.9	91 / 0.9	93 / 0.9	94 / 1.0	96 / 1.0	98 / 1.1	100 / 1.1	101 / 1.2	103 / 1.2	105 / 1.3	107 / 1.4	109 / 1.4	112 / 1.5	114 / 1.6	116 / 1.6	119 / 1.7				
100		100 / 0.9	101 / 1.0	103 / 1.0	105 / 1.1	107 / 1.1	108 / 1.2	110 / 1.3	112 / 1.3	114 / 1.3	117 / 1.4	119 / 1.5	121 / 1.5	123 / 1.6	127 / 1.7						
110		110 / 1.0	111 / 1.0	113 / 1.1	115 / 1.1	117 / 1.2	119 / 1.3	121 / 1.3	123 / 1.4	126 / 1.4	128 / 1.5	130 / 1.6	133 / 1.6								
120		120 / 1.0	121 / 1.1	123 / 1.1	126 / 1.2	128 / 1.3	130 / 1.3	132 / 1.4	134 / 1.5	137 / 1.5	139 / 1.6	143 / 1.7									
130		130 / 1.1	132 / 1.1	134 / 1.2	136 / 1.3	138 / 1.3	141 / 1.4	143 / 1.5	145 / 1.6	148 / 1.6	151 / 1.7										
140		140 / 1.1	142 / 1.2	144 / 1.3	146 / 1.3	149 / 1.4	151 / 1.5	154 / 1.6	156 / 1.6	159 / 1.7											

PO₂	Maximum Operating Depths																			
1.4	187	177	167	159	151	144	138	132	126	121	116	111	107	102	99	95	91	88	85	82
1.5	202	192	182	173	165	157	150	143	137	132	126	121	117	112	108	104	100	97	93	90
1.6	218	207	196	187	178	170	162	156	149	143	137	132	127	122	117	113	109	105	102	99

Instructions for Use
- To determine Equivalent Air Depth (EAD) and partial pressure of oxygen (PO2), start at the FO2 value for the mixture used.
- Move down the FO2 column until you find the depth value that exactly equals or just exceeds the actual dive depth.
- The PO2 for this depth will appear immediately below this number.
- To determine the EAD, move left from the actual depth value to find the Equivalent Air Depth in the far left-hand column.
- As long as the actual dive depth does not exceed the Maximum Operating Depth (MOD) shown at the bottom of the table, it is okay to use the PO2 associated with that MOD.
- Depths shown are in feet of salt water at sea level. Fractional depth values have been rounded down the next shallower integer. Fractional PO2 values are have been rounded upward to the next higher 0.1 bar/ata.

© 2006, SDI/TDI/ERDI - EAD_Imperial_v0317

The Blender

To most people, a blender is a kitchen appliance used to make milkshakes or frozen margaritas. To the nitrox diver, "the blender" is an important person who holds the key to your nitrox diving. Without a properly trained blender, you won't be able to dive nitrox with any degree of confidence.

A nitrox or gas blender has specialized training allowing him or her to fill dive cylinders with the exact gas that divers need for their planned dive. The blender is usually a nitrox diver and has taken a specialized course in gas blending and oxygen management, and there should be a certificate displayed somewhere in or near the blending station showing they have passed.

The blender's job is to supply you with the gas that you ask for when you present your tank to be filled. To this end, the blender makes the required calculations for the cylinder pressure and mixture that you need.

Although we would ideally like to have the exact gas mixture we request, from a practical standpoint it is not always possible. Due to errors in gauges and other factors such as temperature, humidity and the fluctuations in the cells that drive oxygen analyzers can cause variances. For this reason, it is a generally accepted industry standard that as long as the mixture in your tank is within 1% of the target mix, this is sufficient. Given this standard, when you specify EAN32 you may end up with either 31% oxygen or 33% oxygen. Both of these mixtures are still considered within acceptable limits. If you ask for EAN40, and your gear is not cleaned for oxygen service, the blender will be conservative to ensure that you do not end up with a mixture that exceeds 40% oxygen.

The Nitrox Filling Station

There are a number of different types of filling stations that dive centers use for filling nitrox cylinders. Some systems are more sophisticated than others, and some have wider capabilities than others do.

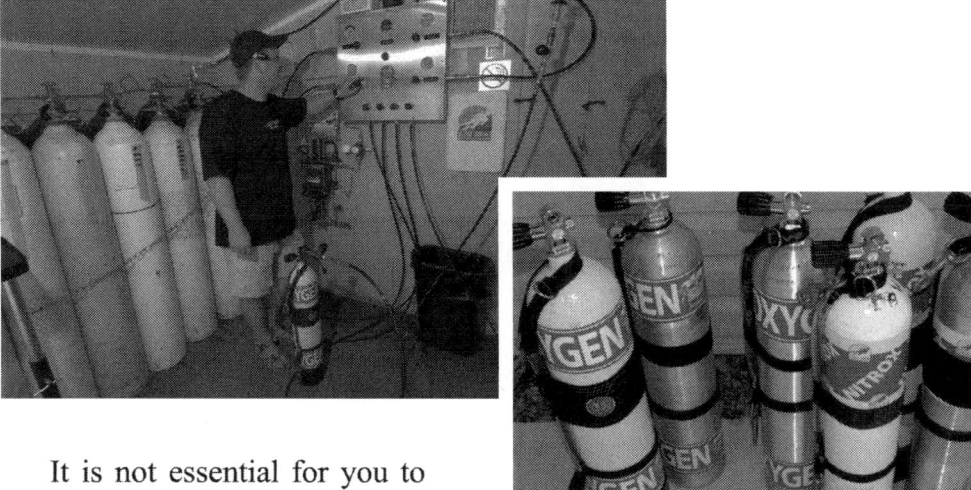

It is not essential for you to know the exact methods used to fill nitrox cylinders, or the terminology that describes each technique. However, if you have dedicated nitrox equipment, i.e., an oxygen clean regulator or cylinders, your cylinders should only be filled at a fill station that is an oxygen clean facility. Anything less will contaminate your equipment with oils that could lead to an explosion or fire if you later use your equipment with nitrox mixtures containing greater than 40% oxygen.

How do you know whether or not a nitrox filling station is oxygen clean? Ask! Don't assume that all filling stations are oxygen clean. One way that you'll know for sure is whether the station can fill nitrox mixtures containing more than 40% oxygen. If they have this capability, then their system must be oxygen clean.

Depending upon the type of filling system in use, the blender may start out by partially filling your cylinder with pure oxygen and then topping off the cylinder with air. Other systems use a semi-permeable membrane, which acts like a filter, to separate nitrogen from oxygen and achieve the gas mixture you desire. Whatever method is used to fill your tank is acceptable, provided you get the correct gas mixture (as long as your system does not need to be oxygen clean).

Signs and labels on the equipment normally identify Nitrox filling stations. In addition, the blender's certification is usually displayed near the fill station, too. If you have any uncertainties about the capabilities of the fill station, ask questions before they fill your tank.

To allow enough time to properly fill a nitrox cylinder, you may want to drop your cylinders off and pick them up later in the day. Most dive centers will request that you leave your cylinders with them for nitrox filling. If you're in a hurry, you may be unable to get your tanks filled exactly when you need them unless you have made prior arrangements.

If you have any uncertainties about the capabilities of the fill station, ask questions before they fill your tank.

Analyzing Your Breathing Gas

Once your tank has been filled, the blender will either check the mixture in your cylinder for you – we advise you to watch – or have you check the mixture yourself. Either method is acceptable, provided you are satisfied that you have the correct gas mixture in your cylinder: because after all, it's you that has to breathe it!

With the oxygen analyzer properly calibrated and the gas flowing from the cylinder, the analyzer should respond to the gas mixture very quickly. Just as it takes a minute or two for the analyzer to stabilize during calibration, it may take a minute for the analyzer to stabilize while taking a reading. You will not get an instantaneous reading of the correct amount. Don't worry about the "lost gas." The flow rate past an oxygen sensor is about 2 litres a minute so waiting for a reading to stabilize uses about two breaths worth of nitrox.

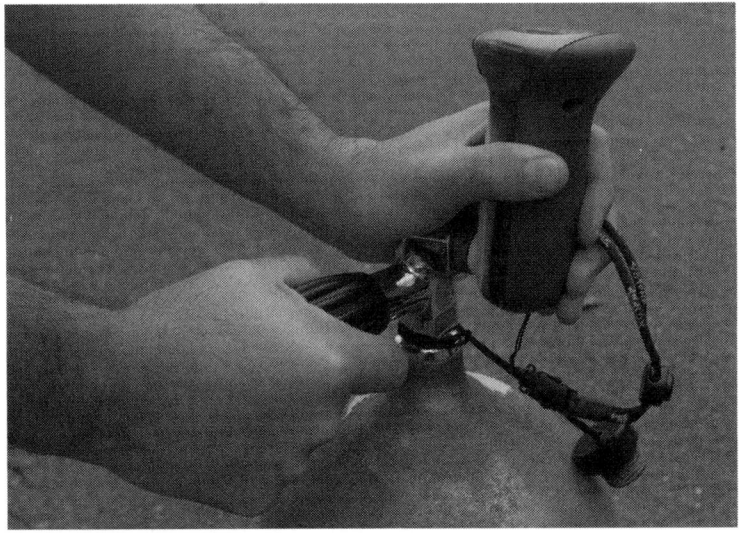

The exact procedure to follow will vary by analyzer (and can be ascertained by following the manufacture's manual), but generally include:

- Begin by connecting your analyzer system to its calibration source, be that a cylinder of pure oxygen, premixed Nitrox or air.

- Oxygen sensors are not only sensitive to oxygen, they can also be affected by the presence of moisture, changes in temperature, sensor age and other factors. Therefore, every time you use an oxygen analyzer, you must calibrate its display against a reference gas whose FO2 is unequiv-

ocal. This can be pure air, oxygen or, lacking these a Nitrox mixture whose FO2 has been verified by at least two other analyzers.

- Most Nitrox divers use pure air as a reference gas, as its FO2 is unequivocal and, being closer to the FO2 of the mixture being analyzed, the margin for error is less than it would be if using pure oxygen as a reference gas.

- Turn the calibration source on. If using an oxygen regulator or other means of adjusting gas flow, adjust the flow rate to that specified by the analyzer manufacturer. Fixed rate meters generally restrict gas flow to a rate of approximately two litres per minute; this is an acceptable rate for most analyzers.

- Once the gas is flowing, and has had the opportunity to displace the air previously in the line, adjust the calibration dial so that it reads either 100.0 percent for oxygen, 20.9 percent for air or the correct percentage for another calibration source, if used. (The calibration dial may be very sensitive; getting the setting within ± 0.1 percent of the target is generally considered adequate.)

- Allow the calibration gas to flow for at least another 30 seconds. Make certain there are no substantial variations in the FO2 reading during this time. If you will be analyzing several cylinders in succession, you only need to calibrate your analyzer once.

- Disconnect the analyzer set-up from the calibration source. Reconnect it to the cylinder you will be analyzing.

- Allow gas to flow until the analyzer reading stabilizes (this may take awhile). Continue to allow gas to flow for another 30 seconds to ensure this reading remains constant.

- Disconnect and store your analyzer in a safe place. Remember to seal the O2 sensor, if separate, in a plastic bag, to protect it from moisture. Oxygen analyzers are delicate instruments and careless handling can damage them very quickly. To complete the process, mark the cylinder contents label with date, FO2, MOD, Limiting PO2, dive operation name and the name or initials of the person conducting the analysis.

Whether the blender analyzes the gas or you do it yourself, the blender will ask you to sign your name in a log indicating that your tanks have been filled, as well as the date, the gas mixture, your certification number, and the pressure in the cylinder. Your signature indicates that you take responsibility for the nitrox that has been delivered to you, and that you are satisfied that your cylinders have been filled properly.

Knowledge Quest

When your tank is filled for nitrox diving, you must take an active role in ensuring you have the correct mixture for your diving. Discuss the following issues with your instructor and be sure you thoroughly understand the concepts presented in this chapter.

1. A _____ is a person whose specialized training allows him to fill cylinders with the exact gas that divers need for their planned dive.

2. What is the acceptable range of accuracy blenders must adhere to when asked to supply a Nitrox mixture with a particular FO2? Plus or minus _____ percent.

3. Prior to using an analyzer, you must _____ it against a reference gas.

4. The *primary* function of a Nitrox fill station log is to transfer _____ from the dive center to the end user.

chapter six

Planning the Nitrox Dive

In this chapter, you'll learn about:

- How to plan a nitrox dive

- How to set a nitrox dive computer

- Nitrox dive computers

- The four things you must do before or during every nitrox dive

No matter what type of diving you do, it's always essential to plan your dive. In nitrox diving, your planning will be only slightly more involved. Planning for a nitrox dive should not take any more time, but it does require a bit of different thinking compared to planning for an air dive.

Check the Availability of Nitrox

While over the past few years Nitrox has become more available all over the world, there are still remote locations where it is not available. The fact that you are reading this manual assumes you are taking or will be taking a course with an SDI dive instructor that is currently filling nitrox cylinders. However if you are traveling to other locations, you will want to check the availability of nitrox prior to arriving to make sure it is available. To do this, SDI recommends you consult your local SDI Dive Center or do some research on the internet. Another popular spot to look for dive centers that provide nitrox is in the director, in the back of popular dive magazines.

Once you have located a store that fills nitrox cylinders, be sure to contact them to check the availability of Nitrox cylinders to rent if you are not bringing yours with you and what they charge for nitrox fills. Most stores charge by the percentage of oxygen included in the mixture. Cylinder fills that contain a higher percentage of oxygen typically cost more than those with a lower percentage. If you are traveling without your own cylinders, most dive centers will rent both the nitrox cylinder with a nitrox fill for slightly more money than that of an air cylinder.

BEFORE EVERY DIVE you must:
- *Know what mix is in your cylinder*
- *Set your mix in your dive computer*

Analyzing the Mix in the Cylinder

In the previous chapter you learned about analyzing your mixes, the importance of why you need to do this, and how to properly label the cylinder. It is important to analyze every cylinder and label the mix on each cylinder. While repeatedly stating this may seem redundant, we know that most nitrox diving accidents occur when the diver grabs the wrong cylinder because it was not properly labeled or fails to analyze the cylinder.

You need to know what is in your cylinder prior to diving so that you can adequately plan your dive, set the mix in your dive computer and avoid an accident.

Set Your Dive Computer

Prior to every nitrox dive, you must check your nitrox dive computer to be sure that it is properly set for the mixture you are using. There are two settings that you must make, one is for the percentage of oxygen that you will be using, and the other is for the maximum PO2 to which you are willing to expose yourself.

Some dive computers, and the manuals that describe them, use the term "fraction of oxygen" or "FO2" rather than the percentage of oxygen in the mix. The fraction of oxygen is the decimal equivalent of the percentage of oxygen in the mix. For example, 32% oxygen is the same thing as .32 FO2.

Different dive computers have different default settings for both the oxygen percentage in the mix and the maximum PO2. These default settings tend to be conservative. In most cases, the default setting for the percentage of oxygen will be 21%. The default setting for PO2 is frequently 1.4. If you fail to change these settings you will not be getting the full benefit of the capabilities of your computer and nitrox.

Today there are numerous different types of dive computers on the market, so your instructor will show you the specific techniques for setting your dive computer. However, here are some general guidelines that you need to keep in mind. Most modern dive computers can be set in 1% increments so that you can adjust the oxygen percentage to the exact mixture in your cylinder. In addition, the maximum PO2 that most computers will allow is 1.6, although a few will allow higher settings.

If you set the oxygen percentage at the correct level for EAN32, but accidentally set your computer to a higher PO2, you will be exposing yourself to dangerous oxygen levels should you also exceed the maximum operating depth of 40 metres / 132 feet for this mixture. Conversely, if you set your computer for EAN32 but change the maximum PO2 to less than 1.6, you will be restricting your maximum depth, which may be desirable under certain conditions.

If you plan to use nitrox but intend to dive conservatively because you are concerned about decompression sickness, you can use an air diving computer and follow its normal limits. If you are using a nitrox computer and want to follow air diving limits, set your oxygen percentage for 21% and your PO2 for 1.6. But you must be careful not to exceed your MOD on your own because the computer is calculating your PO2 as if you are breathing air and not EAN32 as you actually are. Therefore set your plan to go no deeper than 40 metres / 132 feet because your computer alarms will not go off to warn you if you exceed this depth.

Most dive computers will retain the settings that you make at the start of a day of diving for any subsequent dives, until you change the settings in the computer. However, some dive computers will default back to air (21% oxygen) once the computer shuts down. It is also possible that your computer could be accidentally reset to a different gas mixture or partial pressure through contact with other equipment. In addition, more sophisticated computers allow users to change gas mixtures for decompression. For these reasons, it is always wise to recheck the settings on your computer prior to each dive.

If it has been awhile since you last used your dive computer, take the time to re-read the manufacture's manual so you can use it properly. Have the computer with you when you read the manual so you can review any procedures you might have forgotten. Most dive computers have more features than the average diver will use. It is easy to forget how to make some of the more obscure settings. If you are going on an extended dive trip, such as a tropical dive vacation, be sure to take the manual with you, or at the very least, any "cue" cards supplied by the manufacturer.

Maximum Depth Alarm

Some dive computers are equipped with a maximum depth alarm, you should set this for the sport diving limit of 40 metres / 132 feet when diving with EAN32. This will help you to avoid violating your maximum operating depth should you become distracted while taking photos or engaged in some other activity.

Plan Your Maximum Depth and Bottom Time

Use the planning function on your dive computer to scroll through the allowable bottom times for each 3 metre /10 foot increment in your depth, down to 40 metres / 132 feet. If you are on the surface, between dives, use the planning function of your dive computer to check on how long you need to spend on the surface between dives to make the next dive that you want to do.

Remember, the minimum surface interval you should plan between nitrox dives is 30 minutes, and a surface interval of one hour is recommended. Following extended dives, longer surface intervals are recommended.

Nitrox Dive Tables

There are nitrox dive tables that can be used to plan and make nitrox dives. These tables are similar to the air diving tables you may have seen in the past.

Keep in mind that the nitrox no-decompression limits shown here are for single depth, i.e., "square profile" dives. If you compare the dive times listed in the table below to your dive computer's times, your computer will be more conservative for single depth dives. However, your computer calculates multi-level dives automatically for you "on-the-fly", something that is difficult to do with dive tables, ultimately allowing for longer total bottom times.

No Decompression Time Limits for a Single Dive – EAN32											
Depth (m / ft)	9 / 30	12 / 40	15 / 50	18 / 60	22 / 70	25 / 80	28 / 90	30 / 100	33 / 110	36 / 120	40 / 132
NDLS	595	405	200	100	60	50	40	30	30	25	20

Start your dive computer and compare the scrolling dive times that it displays for the no-decompression limits for EAN32 to this table.

Plan Your Dive Conservatively

For dives that are cold or strenuous, avoid diving to the maximum operating depth or shorten your bottom time, or both. Even if you use your dive computer exactly the way it was designed to be used, there is always a slight risk of decompression sickness.

Plan Your Dive with Your Buddy

There are two major reasons your buddy should be diving with the same nitrox mixture that you are using. The first reason is that if your dive buddy fills his tank with air, or a different nitrox mixture that allows him to go deeper without violating his maximum PO2, and dives beyond the MOD for the mixture you are using, you will not be able to go to his aid if he needs help. To do so would violate the MOD of your mixture, putting you in a stressful situation where there is a higher risk that you could suffer from oxygen toxicity.

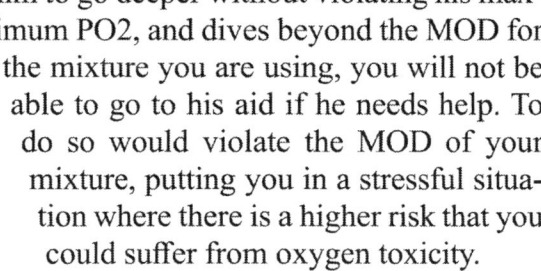

The second reason for diving similar mixes is so you both may extend your bottom time and enjoy the same no decompression limits. This is done to prevent one diver from being required to surface to avoid making a mandatory decompression stop, while the other is still well within no decompression limits.

Plan Your Activity

Before you enter the water, you should know your planned activity for the dive as well as the route you plan for the dive. Remember that exertion can be a triggering factor in oxygen toxicity at the maximum operating depth. Avoid dives where you will be required to swim against strong currents or otherwise exert yourself heavily.

Plan for a Precautionary Decompression Stop

You should plan to make a precautionary decompression stop (safety stop) at the end of every dive. Always plan to leave yourself enough gas to make a stop at a depth of 3 to 6 metres / 10 to 15 feet for 3 and 5 minutes at the end of each dive. Make sure to discuss how and where you will make your safety stop with your dive buddy.

Planning for Emergencies

While in your basic open water class you learned how to plan for an emergency. Most diving related courses will review the things all divers should do in case of an accident. As in all diving, you should always know how to summon assistance if a diving accident should occur. This includes knowing the location of the nearest phone, or making sure the mobile phone you have has a signal where you are.

Plan to make a precautionary decompression stop (safety stop) at the end of every dive.

On charter boats, the captain should have a marine radio to summon assistance in an emergency along with other types of emergency signaling devices. If you are diving from a private boat, it is a good idea to be equipped with either a fixed or hand-held marine radio to use to summon help on Channel 16.

In all pressure related diving injuries (decompression sickness and lung over-pressure injuries), it is important to treat the diver for shock and put them on pure oxygen. This means no matter where you are, be either a charter boat or doing a shore dive, it is important to have the ability to either cool or warm the diver and provide 100 % oxygen. Ultimately, the key to any successful recovery from a pressure related diving accident is to get treatment in a recompression chamber.

It is strongly recommended that every diver have diving accident insurance to cover the high cost of recompression treatment if it should ever become necessary.

Nitrox Dive Check List

- ❏ Analyze your Mix
- ❏ Label your cylinder
- ❏ Set your PO2 and FO2 in your dive computer
- ❏ Do not exceed the MOD of your mix!

Knowledge Quest

Use this chapter as the basis for a discussion with your instructor to help you plan a nitrox dive either as an optional component of your SDI Computer Nitrox class or for future reference when you plan a nitrox dive with your dive buddy.

1. Rather than assume Nitrox will be readily _____ at your destination, you should check ahead of time.

2. If you do not set your dive computer's FO2 prior to every dive, it will typically default to _____ percent.

3. It is important for team members to use the same Nitrox mixture so that they will share a common _____.

chapter seven

Extending Your Nitrox Knowledge-
Continuing Education

In this chapter, you'll learn about:
- What other courses you can take after SDI Computer Nitrox

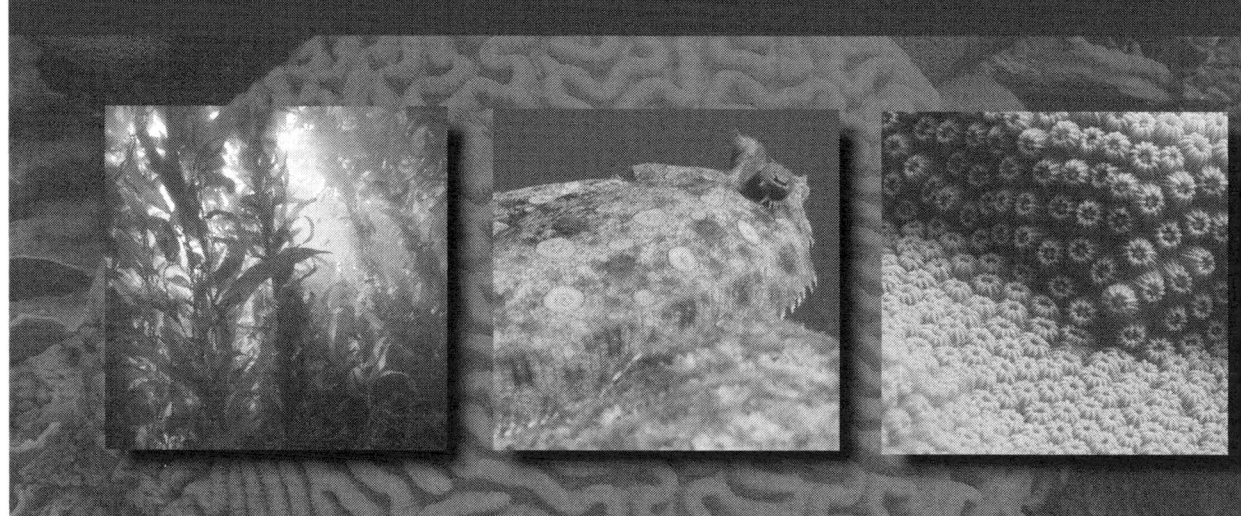

Once you've completed this SDI specialty course, you will probably be ready to push your diving knowledge and skill even further. SDI has a full range of specialty programs to help build your confidence and competence as a recreational diver. What is your particular interest? Wildlife, photography, wrecks, cavern or night diving? Are you interested in joining the SDI leadership team and helping others to dive?

• •

SDI has programs for these specialties and more. In fact, SDI also has a unique specialty: Solo Diver, which is a valuable program for any diver who demands the very highest level of competence from themselves. Talk with your instructor and find out which SDI programs will bring you the most benefit.

Of course, there is much more to nitrox than the mixtures we have covered in this book. For example, you can use an infinite variety of nitrox mixtures. You can use a nitrox rebreather, of which there are several different models. You can also learn to use multiple gas mixtures in a single dive and to use gas mixtures other than oxygen and nitrogen. All of these additional training courses are considered part of the specialty area of diving known as "technical diving".

Technical diving is a type of recreational diving that goes beyond sport diving limits. Typically, it requires additional specialized training, planning techniques and equipment. It provides the diver with capabilities well beyond the limitations of sport diving.

The leader in technical diver training is Technical Diving International (TDI), sister company to Scuba Diving International. Technical Diving International offers courses in nitrox, advanced nitrox, semi-closed circuit rebreathers, fully closed-circuit rebreathers, and Trimix. These courses all build on the information and techniques that you have learned during this course.

TDI Advanced Nitrox Certification

In the SDI Computer Nitrox Diver course you have just completed, you have learned how to use your dive computer to make dives using nitrox mixtures containing 40% oxygen or less. However, there are many other commonly used nitrox mixtures available that can be used for specific applications.

In the TDI Advanced Nitrox Certification course, you will learn to use other commonly used nitrox gas mixtures containing more than 40% oxygen. These "richer" gas mixtures will allow you to extend your bottom times even further than is possible with nitrox mixtures containing 40% oxygen or less, although the depth capabilities for these gases is more limited.

Advanced nitrox training qualifies you to use nitrox gas mixtures containing oxygen in any ratio, as well as 100% oxygen. This course builds on the Nitrox Certification course. In this course, you will also learn to perform the mathematical calculations to compute partial pressures, equivalent air depths, and nitrox dive tables. Your nitrox diving capabilities will be complete. This course is considered a pre-requisite to rebreather training.

TDI Semi-Closed Circuit Rebreather Certification

Semi-closed circuit rebreathers are a specialized type of scuba gear that has become very popular with divers in recent years. The semi-closed circuit rebreather is designed to re-circulate most of each breath you take, by removing the carbon dioxide (CO_2) from your exhaled breath and adding oxygen as it is consumed.

Semi-closed circuit rebreathers for recreational diving are designed to use nitrox as the breathing gas. They allow you to carry a much smaller cylinder of gas, yet greatly extend your bottom time. These are simple mechanical devices that are easy to learn to use.

There are many advantages to using a semi-closed circuit rebreather besides extended bottom time. If you dive from a small boat, using a semi-closed circuit rebreather will save a great deal of space in terms of the size and number of scuba cylinders you must take along to dive.

Another advantage of the semi-closed circuit rebreathers is that they give off very few bubbles and are nearly silent, making it much easier to get closer to certain types of marine life. In addition, the chemical reaction that removes the carbon dioxide warms the breathing gas, helping to maintain body heat in colder waters.

TDI Closed-Circuit Rebreather Certification

Unlike the semi-closed circuit rebreather, fully closed-circuit models do not release any breathing gas bubbles into the water, except during the ascent at the end of the dive. They work in a similar manner to the semi-closed circuit rebreather.

There are two types of fully-closed circuit rebreathers; oxygen rebreathers and electronic rebreathers. Oxygen rebreathers use

100% oxygen and are only used by military divers for shallow water diving, down to depths of 6 metres / 20 feet. This type of rebreather is generally unavailable to the general public and impractical for most sport diving.

Fully-closed circuit electronic rebreathers are more complex than semi-closed circuit units and typically involve some type of on-board electronics to control the gas mixture that you breathe. These rebreathers require extensive training, but they have much broader capabilities, and may be used at extreme depths, hundreds of feet deep. They automatically mix oxygen and nitrogen, or other gas mixtures, to provide exactly the right amount of oxygen, regardless of your depth. They are also much more expensive to purchase, operate, and maintain than semi-closed circuit rebreathers.

Diving with a fully closed-circuit electronic rebreather is considered to be the most sophisticated type of diving that divers do today.

TDI Trimix Certification

Trimix is a gas mixture containing helium, nitrogen, and oxygen. This type of gas mixture is used for diving at depths deeper than 40 metres / 132 feet, down to 60 metres / 200 feet of seawater.

The concept behind Trimix diving is that by replacing most of the nitrogen in the breathing gas with helium, you will be affected less by nitrogen narcosis than you would be using regular air. Trimix diving is almost always decompression diving, which also requires additional training. Decompression diving involves increased risk.

TDI Advanced Trimix Certification

As you might expect, Advanced Trimix training starts where Trimix training ends. This course will qualify you to dive with Trimix down to depths of 100 metres / 330 feet of seawater.

Knowledge Quest

As divers, there is always something new for us to learn. Discuss these technical diving courses with your instructor to gain a greater understanding of other activities you can pursue to build on your nitrox training.

1. Recreational diving activities that take place beyond the commonly accepted sport diving limits are referred to as _____ diving.

2. The TDI Advanced Nitrox Diver course covers the use of Nitrox mixtures ranging from EAN ____ to EAN ____, as well as pure _____.

3. Another advantage of _____ -closed circuit rebreathers is that the chemical reaction that removes the _____ _____ warms the breathing gas, helping to maintain body heat in colder waters.

4. The key reason why technical divers generally prefer Trimix for dives past 40 m/132 ft is that the _____ Trimix contains helps reduce the concentration and, thus, the narcotic effect of the _____ in the gas mixture.

Appendix

Appendix I: Glossary
Appendix II: Tables
Appendix III: An Introduction to Dive Computers

APPENDIX I: Glossary

A

Absolute Pressure: Any measurement of pressure that includes the weight (pressure) of the atmosphere. See *Atmospheres Absolute*.

Air: As used in Nitrox diving, the term air generally refers to "normal" atmospheric air, a gas mixture containing 78 percent nitrogen, 20.9 percent oxygen (usually rounded to 21 percent), plus a collection of trace elements that include argon, carbon dioxide, helium, hydrogen, neon, methane and krypton. The most common methods of creating *Enriched Air Nitrox* involve blending pure oxygen and air in varying amounts.

Ambient Pressure: The surrounding pressure at any depth or altitude.

ATA: See *Atmospheres Absolute*.

ATM: See *Atmospheres*.

Atmospheres: A unit of measure based on the pressure exerted by the weight of the atmosphere at sea level. An atmosphere is defined as 101.325 kPa or 1,013.25 millibars. This equals a pressure of 760.0 millimetres of mercury or 14.696 pounds per square inch (psi).

Atmospheres Absolute (ATA): This term can be used when measuring pressure in atmospheres and including in that measurement the weight of the atmosphere. See *Absolute Pressure*.

B

Bar: A unit of measuring pressure *approximately* equal to one atmosphere (the difference being so negligible as to be considered inconsequential by most divers). A bar is equal to 1,000 millibars or a force of 100,000 Newtons acting on a square metre. Under the International System of Units (*Système International d'Unités* or *SI*), the term *bar* has been depreciated in favor of *Pascals (Pa)*. A bar is equal to 100,000 Pa or 100 kPa. See *Pascals*.

Bends: A colloquial term for *Decompression Sickness (DCS)*. This term came into use in the late 1800s, after caisson workers who were exposed to high pressures developed DCS and would walk in a contortion in order to alleviate some of the pain. Named after a woman's fashion style termed the "Grecian Bends." See *Decompression Sickness*.

Best Mix: A term used to describe a gas mixture whose component gas concentrations are optimized for a given depth. In the case of Nitrox, it means determining a ratio of oxygen and nitrogen that keeps nitrogen exposure as low as possible, while at the same time, not causing users to exceed their desired Limiting PO_2. See *Limiting PO_2*.

Blender: A general term used to describe individuals who possess the required training and certification needed to fill dive cylinders with gas mixtures other than air, or to create such mixtures prior to filling. Blender qualifications vary. An individual who undergoes such training will initially be qualified to blend Nitrox only. With additional training and certification, that qualification can be extended to include filling oxygen and Trimix cylinders. See *Nitrox* and *Trimix*.

Blending: A general term used to describe the various methods used to create *Enriched Air Nitrox*. These methods include: *Partial Pressure Blending* (both inside and outside the end user's cylinder), *Continuous Blending* and *Membrane Systems* (see definitions below).

Boyle's Law: In 1662, Irish physicist and chemist Robert Boyle, then in residence at Oxford, discovered the principles underlying the relationship between gas pressure, volume and density. Referred to commonly as *Boyle's law* (or *Mariotte-Boyle's Law*, in honor of the French physicist who discovered the same principles independently in the late 1800s), this most basic of gas laws states that, given a constant temperature, pressure and volume are inversely proportionate. Mathematically, this can be expressed as $P_1V_1=P_2V_2$.

Buhlmann Tables, Buhlmann Algorithm(s): Swiss scientist Dr. A. A. Buhlmann has been a prolific hyperbaric physiological researcher. He has developed a number of dive tables and algorithms that describe the uptake and release of inert gasses in the body under pressure. Buhlmann algorithms form the basis for a number of dive computers. Also see *Rogers-Powell Algorithm* and *Reduced Gradient Bubble Model*.

C

Central Nervous System (CNS): As used in diving, relates to the brain, brain stem and, in some cases, the spinal cord. The abbreviation *CNS* is used as part of a number of terms, such as *CNS Oxygen Toxicity*.

CNS Oxygen Limit: See *Oxygen Time Limit*.

CNS Oxygen Toxicity: A form of *Oxygen Toxicity* characterized by interference with the operation of the *Central Nervous System* (see definitions below). A diver suffering from CNS oxygen toxicity is at risk of going into convulsions, losing airway control and drowning. CNS oxygen toxicity can be avoided by:

- Establishing a *Limiting PO_2*, based on the specific needs and characteristics of the dive (typically a value of 1.4 or 1.6).
- Establishing a *Maximum Operating Depth* (MOD), based on the Limiting PO_2 and *Fraction of Oxygen* (FO_2), and remaining well within it.
- Remaining well within the *Oxygen Time Limit* for the maximum PO_2 reached during the dive.

(See specific definitions for the terms appearing in italics elsewhere in this Glossary.)

CNS: See *Central Nervous System*.

Commercial Diver: A diver who works underwater for money, usually performing heavy construction work.

Contents Label: A decal or tag used to identify a dive cylinder's gas mixture. Typically includes: FO_2; MOD @ Limiting PO_2 value; analysis date, analyzer's name or initials; and, the name of the dive center where the cylinder was filled or analyzed.

Continuous Blending: A method for creating *Enriched Air Nitrox* in which a carefully metered quantity of oxygen is injected directly into a compressor's intake orifice while the compressor is running. The compressor's output should then be the desired Nitrox mixture. A highly efficient method of creating large quantities of Nitrox — but one that requires a number of specialized equipment components. See *Blending*.

ConVENTID: An acronym for the signs and symptoms of CNS oxygen toxicity. These include:

- Convulsions
- Visual distortions or hallucinations
- Ears or auditory hallucinations
- Nausea
- Tinnitus/Tingling or Twitching
- Irritability or apprehension
- Dizziness or Dyspnea

What is most important to understand is that, by the time any of these signs or symptoms manifest themselves, it may be too late. Thus, rather than concentrate on recognizing and responding to these signs and symptoms, the Nitrox diver's primary focus should be on preventing them.

Cylinder Markings: Within the context of Nitrox diving, these include the *Tank Wrap, Contents Label* and *Oxygen Service Rating Decal* (see definitions above and below).

D

Dalton's Law: Also known as *Dalton's Law of Partial Pressures*, this gas law states that the total pressure exerted by a gas mixture is equal to the sum of the partial pressures of each of its individual component gasses (assuming the gasses do not react to one another. Mathematically, this can be expressed as: $P_{total} = P_1 + P_2 + ... P_n$.

DCS: See *Decompression Sickness*.

Decompression Sickness (DCS): A series of maladies associated with nitrogen coming out of solution in the blood, sometimes as bubbles. This may cause simple pain or be associated with severe neurological effects, such as paralysis, loss of coordination, and loss of bladder or bowel control. Nitrox can help reduce the risk of decompression sickness by exposing divers to lower levels of nitrogen than they would experience when diving to the same depth, for the same lengths of time, using air.

Decompression Stop: A decompression stop takes place when divers halt their ascent at a fixed depth for period of time no less than that specified by their dive tables or computers. This allows inert gas, such as nitrogen, which is coming out of solution as the divers ascend, to do so more slowly, thus reducing the risk of bubble formation and decompression sickness. See *Safety Stop*.

Dive Computer: An electronic device that continuously monitors both time and depth, and compares this data to algorithms which model the average diver's uptake and release of inert gas, such as nitrogen. The computer then informs users whether it is safe to ascend, or whether stage decompression stops are required. Most Nitrox programmable dive computers also monitor divers' exposure to elevated partial pressures of oxygen. A further benefit of dive computers is the fact they generally monitor and help divers control ascent rate far more accurately than divers are capable of doing on their own. Beyond this, dive computers offer an almost dizzying array of features, which will vary depending on make and model.

E

EAD: See *Equivalent Air Depth*,

EAN: See *Nitrox*.

EAN32: See *NOAA Nitrox I*.

EAN36: See *NOAA Nitrox II*.

EANx: A common shorthand for *Enriched Air Nitrox* used when the *Fraction of Oxygen (FO_2)* is unknown (the *x* is a variable representing the missing FO_2 information). When the FO_2 is known, this data takes the place of the *x* (i.e., *EAN32, EAN36*, etc.). *Note:* Divers will sometimes mistakenly denote a Nitrox mixture by including both the *x* and the FO_2 (i.e., *EANx32*). This is the Nitrox equivalent of an oxymoron.

Emergency Response Diving International (ERDI): The public safety arm of Scuba Diving International, specializing in Police, Fire, Rescue and emergency response diving. ERDI divers frequently use SDI and TDI Nitrox Diver training materials. See *Scuba Diving International* and *Technical Diving International*.

Enriched Air Nitrox: See *Nitrox*.

Enriched Air: See *Nitrox*.

Equivalent Air Depth (EAD): A means of comparing air and Nitrox diving depths, based on partial pressures of nitrogen (FN_2s). In so far as *Enriched Air Nitrox* contains lower concentrations of nitrogen than air, divers using it can go to deeper depths before hitting equivalent FN_2 levels. This means, for example, that divers using EAN32 at a depth of 29 m/98 ft will enjoy the same no-decompression limits as air divers will at a depth of 24 m/80 ft. All Nitrox dive tables and computers base themselves on the concept of Equivalent Air Depth.

ERDI: See *Emergency Response Diving International*.

F

Fg: See *Fraction of Gas*.

FN_2: See *Fraction of Nitrogen*.

FO_2: See *Fraction of Oxygen*.

Fraction of Gas (Fg): The percentage of any individual gas present in a mixture, expressed as a decimal value. *Fraction of Nitrogen (FN$_2$)* and *Fraction of Oxygen (FO$_2$)* are examples of Fraction of Gas.

Fraction of Nitrogen (FN2): The percentage of nitrogen present in a gas mixture, expressed as a decimal value. For example, the FN$_2$ of air is 0.78.

Fraction of Oxygen (FO2): The percentage of oxygen present in a gas mixture, expressed as a decimal value. For example, the FO$_2$ of air is .21; the FO$_2$ of Nitrox I (EAN32) is 0.32.

Fuel Cell: See *Oxygen Sensor*.

G

Gauge Pressure: Most pressure gauges, such as your regulator's submersible pressure gauge (SPG), are calibrated to read *0* at sea level. Thus, any pressure readings they display will actually be one atmosphere *less* than absolute pressure. Nitrox divers typically do not use gauge pressure when planning or making Nitrox dives, other than for gas management calculations involving their SPGs. To convert gauge pressure to absolute pressure, add the appropriate atmosphere unit such as 100 kPa for metric or 14.696 psi for imperial.

L

Limiting PO2: Part of planning and making Nitrox dives is establishing a maximum PO$_2$ limit that team members will not exceed. This is generally no more than a PO$_2$ of 1.6 — although most Nitrox divers choose to remain within a value of 1.4, as this may further reduce the risk of CNS oxygen toxicity and can greatly simplify the process of tracking one's exposure to elevated partial pressures of oxygen. Many dive computers are also programmed to sound or display an alarm if users exceed a PO$_2$ of 1.4. See *Maximum Operating Depth*.

M

Maximum Operating Depth (MOD): A maximum depth limit based on *Fraction of Oxygen (FO$_2$)* and the *Limiting PO$_2$*. Divers who remain within their MOD will also remain within their Limiting PO$_2$. MOD is among the information that should appear on any Nitrox cylinder's contents label. Many technical divers also mark MOD prominently on stage and deco bottles, so that buddies will be alerted if they see a fellow team member switching to the wrong bottle at too deep a depth.

Membrane System: A method of creating *Enriched Air Nitrox* in which air is drawn through a special membrane that removes a portion of the nitrogen. Among the most expensive and least efficient methods for creating Nitrox, it is nevertheless well suited for liveaboard dive vessels, where obtaining or storing large oxygen cylinders may be difficult. See *Blending*.

MOD: See *Maximum Operating Depth*.

N

NDL: See *No Decompression Limit*.

Nitrogen Narcosis: Exposure to elevated partial pressures of nitrogen (PN$_2$s) can produce narcotic-like effects. These can impair judgment, slow reaction times and interfere with the ability to perform motor skills. Often compared to alcohol intoxication, nitrogen's effects will actually vary widely from diver to diver, and from day to day. Impairment increases in proportion to depth — although it is generally more noticeable below 30 m/100 ft. At one time, Nitrox was promoted as a means of reducing nitrogen narcosis, as it exposes divers to lower PN$_2$ levels. It has since been established that the oxygen that takes the place of nitrogen in a Nitrox mixture may be equally as narcotic, so divers should not rely on this.

Nitrox Blender: See *Blender*.

Nitrox Decal: See *Tank Wrap*.

Nitrox Filling Station: A dive operation that has the capability to blend Nitrox and fill Nitrox cylinders. This term may also be used to refer to the equipment used to fill Nitrox cylinders, such as a membrane system.

Nitrox Tag: See *Contents Label*.

Nitrox: Nitrox is any gas mixture containing primarily oxygen and nitrogen, with trace elements no greater than those found in air. Strictly speaking, air is a form of Nitrox, as is any oxygen/nitrogen mixture in which the PO$_2$ is *lower* than that of air. More commonly, however, divers use the term *Nitrox* to refer to *Enriched Air Nitrox* — Nitrox in which the PO$_2$ exceeds that of air. Other common terms include *Enriched Air* and *Oxygen Enriched Air*.

No Decompression Limit (NDL): The time divers may spend at any particular depth without having to make mandatory decompression stops during ascent. NDLs may vary from one dive table to another (although generally very similar), and from one dive computer to another. NDLs will vary substantially when divers use Nitrox. For example, a single-dive NDL for 30 m/100 feet may be close to 35 minutes when using EAN32, but just 20 minutes when using air. Such longer no-decompression limits are among the primary reasons divers use Nitrox.

NOAA Nitrox I (EAN32): The most common Nitrox mixture, with an FO$_2$ of 32 percent. Allows divers to remain with the 30 m/100 ft recommended depth limit for sport diving without exceeding a PO$_2$ of 1.4; divers using EAN32 can also go to the maximum depth limit for sport diving (40 m/140 ft) without exceeding a PO$_2$ of 1.6.

NOAA Nitrox II (EAN36): The second most common Nitrox mixture, with an FO$_2$ of 36 percent. An excellent choice for dives above 27 m/90 ft, as it exposes divers at these depths to substantially less nitrogen than air does, while at the same time allowing divers to remain within a PO$_2$ of 1.4.

O

ODL: See *Oxygen Depth Limit* and *Limiting PO$_2$*.

OTL: See *Oxygen Time Limit*.

OTU: See *Oxygen Tolerance Unit*.

Oxygen Analyzer: An instrument used to ascertain and/or verify the oxygen content of a gas cylinder or storage system. An oxygen analyzer system will typically include: a power supply; a means to control gas flow rate from the cylinder within a closed loop; an oxygen sensor; a digital display of FO$_2$; and, an adjustment knob or dial to calibrate the sensor to a reference gas. These components may be separate from one another, or one or more of them may be combined into a single unit. See *Oxygen Sensor*.

Oxygen Clean (O$_2$ Clean): Any item, such as a regulator, cylinder or valve, that has undergone a special cleaning process designed to remove hydrocarbons, grease and other contaminants that could *spontaneously combust* if exposed to concentrations of oxygen in excess of 40 percent, at pressures greater than regulator intermediate pressure. The ability to O$_2$ clean equipment components requires special training and certification. See *Oxygen Compatible* and *Oxygen Service Rated*.

Oxygen Compatible: Lubricants and materials, such as Viton®, which are designed to be used with gas mixtures in which the concentration of oxygen exceeds 40 percent, at pressures greater than regulator intermediate pressure. The neoprene used in most O-rings oxidizes rapidly in oxygen-rich environments and *is not* oxygen compatible. See *Oxygen Clean* and *Oxygen Service Rated*.

Oxygen Depth Limit: See *Limiting PO$_2$* and *Maximum Operating Depth*.

Oxygen Enriched Air: See *Nitrox*.

Oxygen Limit Fraction/Oxygen Limit Index: The percentage of a diver's available Oxygen Time Limit he or she has consumed, or has remaining. This is one of many similar terms dive computer manufacturers use to denote where the user stands in terms of available oxygen time. See also *Oxygen Time Limit*.

Oxygen Poisoning: See *Oxygen Toxicity*.

Oxygen Safe Lubricant: See *Oxygen Compatible*.

Oxygen Sensor: The portion of an oxygen analyzer that reacts to the presence of oxygen. Oxygen sensors are sensitive to changes in moisture and temperature, and their sensitivity can vary over time. For this reason, it is necessary to calibrate the sensor against a reference gas with a known FO_2, such as air. Sensors should be sealed inside air-tight containers, such as a Ziploc® bag, when not in use. See *Oxygen Analyzer*.

Oxygen Service Rated: Equipment that is both *Oxygen Clean* and has been assembled using *Oxygen Compatible* lubricants, O-rings and other materials, is said to be *oxygen service rated*. Any equipment that will be exposed to concentrations of oxygen in excess of 40 percent, at pressures greater than regulator intermediate pressure (such as cylinders used for partial pressure blending) must be oxygen service rated.

Oxygen Service Rating Decal: A decal denoting whether a cylinder has been O_2 *cleaned* and O_2 *service rated* (see individual definitions above). This information may be incorporated as part of the regular tank inspection decal, or appear on a separate label.

Oxygen Time Limit (OTL): The maximum allowable exposure, in minutes, for any given PO_2. The *NOAA Oxygen Exposure Limits for Working Divers* provides time limits for both single dives and 24-hour periods. Most Nitrox-programmable dive computers also employ algorithms designed to help divers remain within acceptable oxygen time limits.

Oxygen Tolerance Unit: A unit of measure used to track a person's exposure to oxygen over extended periods of time, in order to help prevent *Pulmonary Oxygen Toxicity*. Divers are seldom exposed to oxygen long enough to be concerned with OTUs. See *Pulmonary Oxygen Toxicity*.

Oxygen Toxicity: May take either of two forms: *Pulmonary Oxygen Toxicity* and *CNS Oxygen Toxicity* (see definitions above and below). Where pulmonary oxygen toxicity poses almost no threat to recreational Nitrox divers, CNS oxygen toxicity does.

P

Pa: See *Pascals*.

Partial Pressure Blending: The most basic means of creating *Enriched Air Nitrox*. It involves mixing oxygen and air, either in the end user's cylinder, or in large storage cylinders for later transfer to end users' cylinders. Because this method exposes cylinders and valves to pure oxygen at pressures greater than regulator intermediate pressure, it requires that these items be *oxygen clean* and *oxygen service rated* (see definitions above). Although not necessarily the most efficient means of creating Nitrox, this method requires the least specialized equipment, making it well suited for dive operators who do not have a need to create large quantities of Nitrox. See *Blending*.

Partial Pressure: Each component gas in a mixture exerts a *partial pressure* in proportion to its percentage of the whole. For example, air contains approximately 21 percent oxygen. At a depth of two atmospheres, the partial pressure of oxygen would be 21 percent of 2.0 atm, or 0.42 atm PO_2. This has roughly the same physiological effect on our bodies as breathing a mixture containing 42 percent oxygen would at the surface. See *Dalton's Law*.

Partial Pressure of Nitrogen (PN2): A value obtained by multiplying the *Fraction of Nitrogen (FN_2)* by the ambient pressure in atmospheres absolute. See *Partial Pressure*.

Partial Pressure of Oxygen (PO2): A value obtained by multiplying the *Fraction of Oxygen (FO_2)* by the ambient pressure in atmospheres absolute. See *Partial Pressure*.

Pascals (Pa): The means of measuring pressure under the International System of Units (*Système International d'Unités* or *SI*). An atmosphere is defined as 101,325 Pa or 101.325 kPa. An atmosphere is defined as 100,000 Pa or 100 kPa. See *Atmospheres* and *Bar*.

Pg: See *Pressure of a Gas*.

PN_2: See *Partial Pressure of Nitrogen*.

PO_2: See *Partial Pressure of Oxygen*.

Precautionary Decompression Stop: See *Safety Stop*.

Pressure of a Gas: A generic term for the partial pressure of a gas within a mixture. *Partial pressure of oxygen (PO_2)* is an example of a Pressure of a Gas. See *Partial Pressure*.

Pt: See *Total Pressure (Pressure Total)*.

Pulmonary Oxygen Toxicity: A form of oxygen toxicity characterized by exposure to low doses of oxygen over extended periods of time. Sometimes called the *Lorrain-Smith Effect,* for J. Lorrain Smith. Used primarily in medical treatment of individuals, such as burn patients, who spend long periods of time in oxygen-rich environments as part of their therapy. Although pulmonary oxygen toxicity may also be a factor in saturation diving, it is generally something recreational divers need not worry about. See *Oxygen Tolerance Units*.

R

Recompression Chamber: A large metal cylinder, fitted with valves and gauges, designed to treat a diver suffering from decompression sickness, by pressurizing the chamber internally with the diver inside. Also known as a *hyperbaric chamber* or (incorrectly) as a *decompression* chamber.

Recompression Treatment: A specified procedure for pressurizing a diver in a recompression chamber and slowly decompressing the diver while he (generally) breathes pure oxygen.

Reduced Gradient Bubble Model (RGBM): A popular inert-gas uptake/release model used in some dive tables and computers.

Residual Nitrogen Time (RNT): The term used to describe the amount of dissolved nitrogen in the diver's body as a result of previous dives. Must be taken into account when planning repetitive dives using dive tables. The amount of time will depend on the previous dive's depth and time, the *Surface Interval Time (SIT)* as well as the planned new dive depth.

RGBM: See *Reduced Gradient Bubble Model*.

Rogers-Powell Algorithm: A popular inert-gas uptake/release model used in some dive tables and computers.

RNT: See *Residual Nitrogen Time*.

SafeAir®: A registered trademark used by some training organizations and instructors to describe Nitrox. (*Note:* Nitrox by any other name is still Nitrox.)

S

Safety Stop: A precautionary decompression stop made, even though not required by a dive table or computer. Safety stops typically take place between 3-6 m/10-20 ft, for from three to five minutes. Even though not required, safety stops can substantially reduce the likelihood of decompression sickness and are therefore strongly recommended for all but the shallowest dives.

Scuba Diving International (SDI): The sport diving arm of Technical Diving International. See *Technical Diving International, Emergency Response Diving International*.

Sensor: See *Oxygen Sensor*.

SI, SIT: See *Surface Interval Time*.

Surface Interval, Surface Interval Time: The time divers spend at the surface between dives. During surface intervals, divers off gas substantial amounts of inert gas, which will allow them to make longer repetitive dives. Divers will also recover, at least partially, from their exposure to elevated partial pressures of oxygen during previous dives. A benefit of dive computers is that they automatically track and make allowances for the positive effects of surface intervals.

T

Tank Wrap: Common name for the large, green-and-yellow encircling decal commonly used to identify cylinders that may contain oxygen/nitrogen gas mixtures with a FO_2s greater than that of air. Nitrox tank wraps signify that, because the cylinder *may* contain a gas mixture with an FO_2 greater than 21 percent, its contents *must* be analyzed prior to use. It does not necessarily mean, however, that the cylinder is O_2 clean or O_2 service rated; this is denoted by a separate decal. See *Cylinder Markings, Oxygen Service Rating Decal.*

TDI: See *Technical Diving International.*

Technical Diving: Any form of recreational diving that involves planned stage decompression, depths beyond 40 m/132 ft, or the use of gasses other than a single mixture of air or Nitrox. Common technical diving activities include: wreck diving beyond sport diving depth and time limits, or advanced wreck penetration; cave diving; and rebreather diving. Technical diving almost always involves the use of gas mixtures other than air, making Nitrox Diver training an important prerequisite. All technical diving requires special training, certification and equipment. See *Technical Diving International.*

Technical Diving International (TDI): The technical diving arm of Scuba Diving International. The world's largest and most widely recognized technical diver training organization, offering a wide variety of technical courses. See *Scuba Diving International* and *Emergency Response Diving International.*

Total Pressure: The total pressure exerted on an object at a specific depth, including the weight (pressure) of the atmosphere. This term is also used as the sum of all the partial pressures in a gas mixtures. Written as P_t. See *Absolute Pressure* and *Dalton's Law.*

Trimix: A gas mixture containing three gases — usually oxygen, nitrogen and helium. Because helium does not have the potential narcotic effect of nitrogen and oxygen, and because it can help dilute the potentially toxic effect of oxygen at great depths, without contributing to narcosis, Trimix is the gas of choice for deeper technical dives. Trimix diving requires special training, certification and equipment. Nitrox Diver training is an important prerequisite.

Want more?

Night Navigation and Limited Visibility

Deeper Diving with Dive Computers

Wreck, Boat and Drift Diving

Dry Suit Diving

Solo Diving

Your SDI instructor or facility can satisfy your appetite for diving.

APPENDIX II: Tables

This section contains a compilation of the various charts and tables you've seen throughout this manual. These provide information on PO2s, MODs, EADs and Oxygen Time Limits. The charts appearing on last three pages of this section combine most of this information into a single, two sided table that is available in a waterproof version you can take with you under water.

PO2	Single Limit Dive Time in Minutes	24 Hour Limit Time in Minutes
0.6	720	720
0.7	540	540
0.8	450	450
0.9	360	360
1.0	300	300
1.1	240	270
1.2	210	240
1.3	180	210
1.4	150	180
1.5	120	180
1.6	45	150

NOAA Oxygen Exposure Limits for Working Divers

Appendix II | Tables

Equivalent Air Depths, Partial Pressures of Oxygen and Maximum Operating Depths

EAD	FO₂ 21%	22%	23%	24%	25%	26%	27%	28%	29%	30%	31%	32%	33%	34%	35%	36%	37%	38%	39%	40%
9	9 0.4	9 0.5	9 0.5	9 0.5	10 0.5	10 0.6	10 0.6	10 0.6	11 0.7	11 0.7	11 0.7	12 0.8	12 0.8	12 0.8	13 0.9	13 0.9	13 0.9	14 1.0	14 1.0	15 1.0
12	12 0.5	12 0.5	12 0.6	13 0.6	13 0.6	13 0.7	13 0.7	14 0.7	14 0.7	14 0.8	15 0.8	15 0.8	15 0.9	16 0.9	16 1.0	17 1.0	17 1.0	18 1.1	18 1.1	18 1.2
15	15 0.6	15 0.6	15 0.6	15 0.6	16 0.7	16 0.7	17 0.8	17 0.8	17 0.8	18 0.9	18 0.9	19 1.0	19 1.0	19 1.0	20 1.1	20 1.1	21 1.1	21 1.2	22 1.3	22 1.3
18	18 0.6	18 0.7	18 0.7	19 0.7	19 0.8	19 0.8	20 0.9	20 0.9	21 0.9	21 1.0	22 1.0	22 1.1	23 1.1	23 1.2	24 1.2	24 1.3	25 1.3	25 1.4	26 1.5	26 1.5
21	21 0.7	21 0.7	21 0.8	22 0.8	22 0.8	23 0.9	23 0.9	24 1.0	24 1.0	24 1.0	25 1.1	26 1.1	26 1.2	27 1.3	27 1.3	28 1.4	28 1.5	29 1.5	30 1.6	30 1.6
24	24 0.8	24 0.8	24 0.8	25 0.9	25 0.9	26 1.0	26 1.0	27 1.1	27 1.1	28 1.2	28 1.2	29 1.3	30 1.4	30 1.4	31 1.5	31 1.5	32 1.6	33 1.7	34 1.8	34 1.8
27	27 0.8	27 0.9	27 0.9	28 1.0	28 1.0	29 1.1	30 1.1	30 1.2	31 1.2	31 1.3	32 1.4	32 1.4	33 1.5	34 1.5	34 1.6	35 1.7	36 1.8			
30	30 0.9	30 0.9	31 1.0	31 1.0	32 1.1	32 1.1	33 1.2	33 1.3	34 1.3	35 1.4	35 1.4	36 1.5	37 1.6	37 1.6	38 1.7					
33	33 1.0	33 1.0	34 1.1	34 1.1	35 1.2	35 1.2	36 1.3	37 1.4	37 1.4	38 1.5	39 1.6	39 1.6	40 1.7	41 1.8						
36	36 1.0	36 1.1	37 1.1	37 1.2	38 1.2	39 1.3	39 1.4	40 1.4	41 1.5	41 1.6	42 1.7	43 1.7								
39	39 1.1	39 1.1	40 1.2	40 1.2	41 1.3	42 1.4	43 1.5	43 1.5	44 1.6	45 1.7										
42	42 1.1	42 1.2	43 1.3	44 1.3	44 1.4	45 1.5	46 1.6	47 1.6	47 1.7											

Maximum Operating Depths

PO₂	21%	22%	23%	24%	25%	26%	27%	28%	29%	30%	31%	32%	33%	34%	35%	36%	37%	38%	39%	40%
1.4	56	53	50	48	46	43	41	40	38	36	35	33	32	31	30	28	27	26	25	25
1.5	61	58	55	52	50	47	45	43	41	40	38	36	35	34	32	31	30	29	28	27
1.6	66	62	59	56	54	51	49	47	45	43	41	40	38	37	35	34	33	32	31	30

Instructions for Use
- To determine Equivalent Air Depth (EAD) and partial pressure of oxygen (PO2), start at the FO2 value for the mixture used.
- Move down the FO2 column until you find the depth value that exactly equals or just exceeds the actual dive depth.
- The PO2 for this depth will appear immediately below this number.
- To determine the EAD, move left from the actual depth value to find the Equivalent Air Depth in the far left-hand column.
- As long as the actual dive depth does not exceed the Maximum Operating Depth (MOD) shown at the bottom of the table, it is okay to use the PO2 associated with that MOD.
- Depths shown are in Meters of salt water at sea level. Fractional depth values have been rounded down to the next shallower integer. Fractional PO2 values are have been rounded upward to the next higher 0.1 bar/ata.

WARNING

Susceptibility to decompression sickness and oxygen toxicity can vary from person to person, and from day to day • No dive table, computer or planning device can guarantee that — even if used correctly — you will not suffer from one or both of these problems • therefore, the user must assume all risks associated with the use of this product • Caution is recommended

© 2006, SDI/TDI/ERDI • EAD_Metric_v0517   Item #: 110511

Equivalent Air Depths, Partial Pressures of Oxygen and Maximum Operating Depths

EAD / FO₂	21%	22%	23%	24%	25%	26%	27%	28%	29%	30%	31%	32%	33%	34%	35%	36%	37%	38%	39%	40%
30	30 / 0.4	30 / 0.5	31 / 0.5	32 / 0.5	33 / 0.5	34 / 0.6	35 / 0.6	36 / 0.6	37 / 0.7	38 / 0.7	39 / 0.7	40 / 0.7	41 / 0.8	42 / 0.8	43 / 0.9	44 / 0.9	46 / 0.9	47 / 1.0	48 / 1.0	49 / 1.0
40	40 / 0.5	40 / 0.5	41 / 0.6	42 / 0.6	43 / 0.6	44 / 0.7	46 / 0.7	47 / 0.7	48 / 0.8	49 / 0.8	50 / 0.8	51 / 0.9	53 / 0.9	54 / 0.9	55 / 1.0	57 / 1.0	58 / 1.1	60 / 1.1	61 / 1.2	63 / 1.2
50	50 / 0.6	51 / 0.6	52 / 0.6	53 / 0.7	54 / 0.7	55 / 0.7	56 / 0.8	58 / 0.8	59 / 0.9	60 / 0.9	62 / 0.9	63 / 1.0	64 / 1.0	66 / 1.1	67 / 1.1	69 / 1.2	71 / 1.2	72 / 1.3	74 / 1.3	76 / 1.4
60	60 / 0.6	61 / 0.7	62 / 0.7	63 / 0.7	64 / 0.8	66 / 0.8	67 / 0.9	69 / 0.9	70 / 1.0	71 / 1.0	73 / 1.0	75 / 1.1	76 / 1.1	78 / 1.2	80 / 1.2	81 / 1.3	83 / 1.4	85 / 1.4	87 / 1.5	89 / 1.5
70	70 / 0.7	71 / 0.7	72 / 0.8	74 / 0.8	75 / 0.9	76 / 0.9	78 / 1.0	80 / 1.0	81 / 1.0	83 / 1.1	84 / 1.1	86 / 1.2	88 / 1.3	90 / 1.3	92 / 1.4	94 / 1.4	96 / 1.5	98 / 1.6	100 / 1.6	102 / 1.6
80	80 / 0.8	81 / 0.8	82 / 0.9	84 / 0.9	86 / 0.9	87 / 1.0	89 / 1.0	91 / 1.1	92 / 1.2	94 / 1.2	96 / 1.3	98 / 1.3	100 / 1.4	102 / 1.4	104 / 1.5	106 / 1.6	108 / 1.6	110 / 1.7	113 / 1.8	
90	90 / 0.8	91 / 0.9	93 / 0.9	94 / 1.0	96 / 1.0	98 / 1.1	100 / 1.1	101 / 1.2	103 / 1.2	105 / 1.3	107 / 1.4	109 / 1.4	112 / 1.5	114 / 1.6	116 / 1.6	119 / 1.7				
100	100 / 0.9	101 / 0.9	103 / 1.0	105 / 1.1	107 / 1.1	108 / 1.2	110 / 1.2	112 / 1.3	114 / 1.3	117 / 1.4	119 / 1.5	121 / 1.5	123 / 1.6	127 / 1.7						
110	110 / 1.0	111 / 1.0	113 / 1.1	115 / 1.1	117 / 1.2	119 / 1.2	121 / 1.3	123 / 1.4	126 / 1.4	128 / 1.5	130 / 1.6	133 / 1.6								
120	120 / 1.0	121 / 1.1	123 / 1.1	126 / 1.2	128 / 1.3	130 / 1.3	132 / 1.4	134 / 1.5	137 / 1.5	139 / 1.6	143 / 1.7									
130	130 / 1.1	132 / 1.1	134 / 1.2	136 / 1.3	138 / 1.3	141 / 1.4	143 / 1.5	145 / 1.6	148 / 1.6	151 / 1.7										
140	140 / 1.1	142 / 1.2	144 / 1.3	146 / 1.4	149 / 1.4	151 / 1.5	154 / 1.6	156 / 1.6	159 / 1.7											

Maximum Operating Depths

PO₂	21%	22%	23%	24%	25%	26%	27%	28%	29%	30%	31%	32%	33%	34%	35%	36%	37%	38%	39%	40%
1.4	187	177	167	159	151	144	138	132	126	121	116	111	107	102	99	95	91	88	85	82
1.5	202	192	182	173	165	157	150	143	137	132	126	121	117	112	108	104	100	97	93	90
1.6	218	207	196	187	178	170	162	156	149	143	137	132	127	122	117	113	109	105	102	99

Instructions for Use
- To determine Equivalent Air Depth (EAD) and partial pressure of oxygen (PO2), start at the FO2 value for the mixture used.
- Move down the FO2 column until you find the depth value that exactly equals or just exceeds the actual dive depth.
- The PO2 for this depth will appear immediately below this number.
- To determine the EAD, move left from the actual depth value to find the Equivalent Air Depth in the far left-hand column.

- As long as the actual dive depth does not exceed the Maximum Operating Depth (MOD) shown at the bottom of the table, it is okay to use the PO2 associated with that MOD.
- Depths shown are in feet of salt water at sea level. Fractional depth values have been rounded down the next shallower integer. Fractional PO2 values are have been rounded upward to the next higher 0.1 bar/ata.

WARNING
Susceptibility to decompression sickness and oxygen toxicity can vary from person to person, and from day to day - No dive table, computer or planning device can guarantee that — even if used correctly — you will not suffer from one or both of these problems - therefore, the user must assume all risks associated with the use of this product - Caution is recommended

© 2006, SDI/TDI/ERDI • EAD_Imperial_v0317
Item#: 110510

Appendix II | Tables

Oxygen Exposure Time Limits (CNS "Clock")

PO₂	Single Dive Limit / 24-Hour Limit	1	2	3	4	5	10	15	20	25	30	35	40	45	50	55	60	Time in Minutes
0.6	720 / 720	1%/1%	1%/1%	1%/1%	1%/1%	1%/1%	1%/1%	2%/2%	3%/3%	3%/3%	4%/4%	5%/5%	6%/6%	6%/6%	7%/7%	8%/8%	8%/8%	
0.7	540 / 540	1%/1%	1%/1%	1%/1%	1%/1%	1%/1%	2%/2%	3%/3%	4%/4%	5%/5%	6%/6%	6%/6%	7%/7%	8%/8%	9%/9%	10%/10%	11%/11%	
0.8	450 / 450	1%/1%	1%/1%	1%/1%	1%/1%	1%/1%	2%/2%	3%/3%	4%/4%	6%/6%	7%/7%	8%/8%	9%/9%	10%/10%	11%/11%	12%/12%	13%/13%	
0.9	360 / 360	1%/1%	1%/1%	1%/1%	1%/1%	1%/1%	3%/3%	4%/4%	6%/6%	7%/7%	8%/8%	10%/10%	11%/11%	13%/13%	14%/14%	15%/15%	17%/17%	
1.0	300 / 300	1%/1%	1%/1%	1%/1%	1%/1%	2%/2%	3%/3%	5%/5%	7%/7%	8%/8%	10%/10%	12%/12%	13%/13%	15%/15%	17%/17%	18%/18%	20%/20%	
1.1	240 / 270	1%/1%	1%/1%	1%/1%	2%/1%	2%/2%	4%/4%	6%/6%	8%/7%	10%/9%	13%/11%	15%/13%	17%/15%	19%/17%	21%/19%	23%/20%	25%/22%	
1.2	210 / 240	1%/1%	1%/1%	1%/1%	2%/1%	2%/2%	5%/4%	7%/6%	10%/8%	12%/10%	14%/13%	17%/15%	19%/17%	21%/19%	24%/21%	26%/23%	29%/25%	
1.3	180 / 210	1%/1%	1%/1%	2%/1%	2%/2%	3%/2%	6%/5%	8%/7%	11%/10%	14%/12%	17%/14%	19%/17%	22%/19%	25%/21%	28%/24%	31%/26%	33%/29%	
1.4	150 / 180	1%/1%	1%/1%	2%/1%	3%/2%	3%/3%	7%/6%	10%/8%	13%/11%	17%/14%	20%/17%	23%/19%	27%/22%	30%/25%	33%/28%	37%/31%	40%/33%	
1.5	120 / 180	1%/1%	2%/1%	3%/2%	3%/2%	4%/3%	8%/6%	13%/8%	17%/11%	21%/14%	25%/17%	29%/19%	33%/22%	38%/25%	42%/28%	46%/31%	50%/33%	
1.6	45 / 150	2%/1%	4%/1%	7%/2%	9%/3%	11%/3%	22%/7%	33%/10%	44%/13%	56%/17%	67%/20%	78%/23%	89%/27%	100%/30%	— / 33%	— / 37%	— / 40%	

Instructions for Use

- This chart allows you to quickly calculate what percentage of your total oxygen exposure limits you have consumed on each dive.
- To use the chart, being by determining the partial pressure of oxygen (PO2) experienced at the deepest point during the dive (see reverse side).
- Find this PO2 value in the left-hand column, and then move across horizontally until you find the column that matches the length of the dive, in minutes.
- The numbers in each box represent the percentage of the total time limits consumed during the dive. The topmost value represents the percentage of the single-dive limit consumed, the lowermost value represents the percentage of the 24-hour limit consumed.

- You can combine percentage values from different columns to determine totals that are precise to the minute. For example, for a 67-minute dive, add the percentages from the 60, 5 and 2 minute columns.
- For multiple dives separated by sufficient surface intervals, it may be possible to "recover" some of the time limits consumed on previous dives. Consult the TDI advanced Nitrox Diver course manual for more information.
- Time values in this chart are based on the *NOAA Oxygen Exposure Time Limits for Working Divers*. Fractional percentage values have been rounded to the nearest whole number, with a minimum value of one percent.

⚠ WARNING

Susceptibility to decompression sickness and oxygen toxicity can vary from person to person, and from day to day. No dive table, computer or planning device can guarantee that — even if used correctly — you will not suffer from one or both of these problems. Therefore, the user must assume all risks associated with the use of this product. Caution is recommended.

© 2006, SDI/TDI/ERDI - CNS Table

INTERNATIONAL TRAINING
18 Elm Street Topsham, Maine 04086

Depth, Mix and PO₂ Chart
Air thru EAN .40   METRIC (MSW)

PARTIAL PRESSURE OF OXYGEN AND SINGLE DIVE EXPOSURE TIME LIMITS IN MINUTES

PO2	O2 Time	.21	.22	.23	.24	.25	.26	.27	.28	.29	.30	.31	.32	.33	.34	.35	.36	.37	.38	.39	.40
1.0	300	37.6	35.4	33.4	31.6	30.0	28.4	27.0	25.7	24.4	23.3	22.2	21.2	20.3	19.4	18.5	17.7	17.0	16.3	15.6	15.0
1.1	240	42.3	40.0	37.8	35.8	34.0	32.3	30.7	29.2	27.9	26.6	25.4	24.3	23.3	22.3	21.4	20.5	19.7	18.9	18.2	17.5
1.2	210	47.1	44.5	42.1	40.0	38.0	36.1	34.4	32.8	31.3	30.0	28.7	27.5	26.3	25.2	24.2	23.3	22.4	21.5	20.7	20.0
1.3	180	51.9	49.0	46.5	44.1	42.0	40.0	38.1	36.4	34.8	33.3	31.9	30.6	29.3	28.2	27.1	26.1	25.1	24.2	23.3	22.5
1.4	150	56.6	53.6	50.8	48.3	46.0	43.8	41.8	40.0	38.2	36.6	35.1	33.7	32.4	31.1	30.0	28.8	27.8	26.8	25.8	25.0
1.5	120	61.4	58.1	55.2	52.5	50.0	47.6	45.5	43.5	41.7	40.0	38.3	36.8	35.4	34.1	32.8	31.6	30.5	29.4	28.4	27.5
1.6	45	66.1	62.7	59.5	56.6	54.0	51.5	49.2	47.1	45.1	43.3	41.6	40.0	38.4	37.0	35.7	34.4	33.2	32.1	31.0	30.0

HOW TO USE THIS TABLE: This table provides the maximum allowable oxygen exposures for different oxygen mixtures at PO2s up to 1.6. The left hand column shows the PO2 values. The next column to the right shows oxygen exposures in minutes. Each of the columns for PO2 values list the depths at which the mixture in that column reaches a range of PO2 values from 1.0 to 1.6.

EXAMPLE: With a PO2 of 1.6, how long can you spend at 34.4 meters breathing EAN 36? Answer: 45 minutes.

INTERNATIONAL TRAINING
18 Elm Street Topsham, Maine 04086

Depth, Mix and PO₂ Chart
Air thru EAN .40   Imperial (FSW)

PARTIAL PRESSURE OF OXYGEN AND SINGLE DIVE EXPOSURE TIME LIMITS IN MINUTES

PO2	O2 Time	.21	.22	.23	.24	.25	.26	.27	.28	.29	.30	.31	.32	.33	.34	.35	.36	.37	.38	.39	.40
1.0	300	124	117	110	104	99	93	89	84	80	77	73	70	67	64	61	58	56	53	51	49
1.1	240	139	132	124	118	112	106	101	96	92	88	84	80	77	73	70	67	65	62	60	57
1.2	210	155	147	139	132	125	119	113	108	103	99	94	90	87	83	80	77	74	71	68	66
1.3	180	171	162	153	145	138	132	125	120	114	110	105	101	97	93	89	86	82	79	77	74
1.4	150	187	177	167	159	151	144	138	132	126	121	116	111	107	102	99	95	91	88	85	82
1.5	120	202	192	182	173	165	157	150	143	137	132	126	121	117	112	108	104	100	97	93	90
1.6	45	218	207	196	187	178	170	162	155	149	143	137	132	127	122	117	113	109	105	102	99

HOW TO USE THIS TABLE: This table provides the maximum allowable oxygen exposures for different oxygen mixtures at PO2s up to 1.6. The left hand column shows the PO2 values. The next column to the right shows oxygen exposures in minutes. Each of the columns for PO2 values list the depths at which the mixture in that column reaches a range of PO2 values from 1.0 to 1.6.

EXAMPLE: With a PO2 of 1.6, how long can you spend at 113 feet breathing EAN 36? Answer: 45 minutes.

Appendix II | Tables

GROUP DESIGNATION
*Highest repetitive group that can be achieved at this depth regardless of bottom time.

Depth (feet)	No-Deco Limits (min)	A	B	C	D	E	F	G	H	I	J	K	L	M	N	O	Z
10	Unlimited	57	101	158	245	426	*										
15	Unlimited	36	60	88	121	163	217	297	449	*							
20	Unlimited	26	43	61	82	106	133	165	205	256	330	461	*				
25	1102	20	33	47	62	78	97	117	140	166	198	236	285	354	469	992	1102
30	371	17	27	38	50	62	76	91	107	125	145	167	193	223	260	307	371
35	232	14	23	32	42	52	63	74	87	100	115	131	148	168	190	215	232
40	163	12	20	27	36	44	53	63	73	84	95	108	121	135	151	163	
45	125	11	17	24	31	39	46	55	63	72	82	92	102	114	125		
50	92	9	15	21	28	34	41	48	56	63	71	80	89	92			
55	74	8	14	19	25	31	37	43	50	56	63	71	74				
60	63	7	12	17	22	28	33	39	45	51	57	63					
70	48	6	10	14	19	23	28	32	37	42	47	48					
80	39	5	9	12	16	20	24	28	32	36	39						
90	33	4	7	11	14	17	21	24	28	31	33						
100	25	4	6	9	12	15	18	21	25								
110	20	3	6	8	11	14	16	19	20								
120	15	3	5	7	10	12	15										
130	12	2	4	6	9	11	12										
140	10	2	4	5	8	10											
150	8		3	5	7	8											
160	7		3	5	6	7											
170	6			4	5	6											
180	6			4	5	6											
190	5			3	5												

WARNING: Even strict compliance with these charts will not guarantee avoidance of decompression sickness. Conservative usage is strongly recommended.

*Dives following surface intervals longer than this are not repetitive dives. Use actual bottom times in the Air Decompression Tables to compute decompression for such dives.

Surface Interval Table (Repetitive Group)

A	0:10 – 2:20*						
B	0:10 – 1:16	1:17 – 3:36*					
C	0:10 – 0:55	0:56 – 2:11	2:12 – 4:31*				
D	0:10 – 0:52	0:53 – 1:47	1:48 – 3:03	3:04 – 5:23*			
E	0:10 – 0:52	0:53 – 1:44	1:45 – 2:39	2:40 – 3:55	3:56 – 6:15*		
F	0:10 – 0:52	0:53 – 1:44	1:45 – 2:37	2:38 – 3:31	3:32 – 4:48	4:49 – 7:08*	
G	0:10 – 0:52	0:53 – 1:44	1:45 – 2:37	2:38 – 3:29	3:30 – 4:23	4:24 – 5:40	5:41 – 8:00*
H	0:10 – 0:52	0:53 – 1:44	1:45 – 2:37	2:38 – 3:29	3:30 – 4:22	4:23 – 5:16	5:17 – 6:33 / 6:52 – 8:52*
I	0:10 – 0:52	0:53 – 1:44	1:45 – 2:37	2:38 – 3:29	3:30 – 4:21	4:22 – 5:13	5:14 – 6:08 / 6:09 – 7:25 / 7:24 – 9:44*
J	0:10 – 0:52	0:53 – 1:44	1:45 – 2:37	2:38 – 3:29	3:30 – 4:21	4:22 – 5:13	5:14 – 6:06 / 6:07 – 7:00 / 7:01 – 8:16 / 8:17 – 10:36*
K	0:10 – 0:52	0:53 – 1:44	1:45 – 2:37	2:38 – 3:29	3:30 – 4:21	4:22 – 5:13	5:14 – 6:05 / 6:06 – 6:58 / 6:59 – 7:52 / 7:53 – 9:09 / 9:10 – 11:29*
L	0:10 – 0:52	0:53 – 1:44	1:45 – 2:37	2:38 – 3:29	3:30 – 4:21	4:22 – 5:13	5:14 – 6:05 / 6:06 – 6:58 / 6:59 – 7:50 / 7:51 – 8:44 / 8:45 – 10:01 / 10:02 – 12:21*
M	0:10 – 0:52	0:53 – 1:44	1:45 – 2:37	2:38 – 3:29	3:30 – 4:21	4:22 – 5:13	5:14 – 6:05 / 6:06 – 6:58 / 6:59 – 7:50 / 7:51 – 8:42 / 8:43 – 9:37 / 9:38 – 10:53 / 10:54 – 13:13*
N	0:10 – 0:52	0:53 – 1:44	1:45 – 2:37	2:38 – 3:29	3:30 – 4:21	4:22 – 5:13	5:14 – 6:05 / 6:06 – 6:58 / 6:59 – 7:50 / 7:51 – 8:42 / 8:43 – 9:34 / 9:35 – 10:29 / 10:30 – 11:46 / 11:47 – 14:05*
O	0:10 – 0:52	0:53 – 1:44	1:45 – 2:37	2:38 – 3:29	3:30 – 4:21	4:22 – 5:13	5:14 – 6:05 / 6:06 – 6:58 / 6:59 – 7:50 / 7:51 – 8:42 / 8:43 – 9:34 / 9:35 – 10:27 / 10:28 – 11:20 / 11:21 – 12:37 / 12:38 – 14:58*
Z	0:10 – 0:52	0:53 – 1:44	1:45 – 2:37	2:38 – 3:29	3:30 – 4:21	4:22 – 5:13	5:14 – 6:05 / 6:06 – 6:58 / 6:59 – 7:50 / 7:51 – 8:42 / 8:43 – 9:34 / 9:35 – 10:27 / 10:28 – 11:19 / 11:20 – 12:13 / 12:14 – 13:30 / 13:31 – 15:50*

Instructions: Locate the diver's repetitive group designation from his previous dive along the diagonal line above the table. Read horizontally to the interval in which the diver's surface interval lies.

Next, read vertically downward to the new repetitive group designation. Continue downward in this same column to the row that represents the depth of the repetitive dive. The time given at the intersection is residual nitrogen time, in minutes, to be applied to the repetitive dive.

Repetitive Group at the End of the Surface Interval

Repetitive Dive Depth (feet)	Z	O	N	M	L	K	J	I	H	G	F	E	D	C	B	A
10	**	**	**	**	**	**	**	**	**	**	**	427	246	159	101	58
15	**	**	**	**	**	**	**	**	**	450	298	218	164	122	89	61	37
20	**	**	**	**	**	462	331	257	206	166	134	106	83	62	44	27
25	†	†	470	354	286	237	198	167	141	118	98	79	63	48	34	21
30	372	308	261	224	194	168	146	126	108	92	77	63	51	39	28	18
35	245	216	191	169	149	132	116	101	88	75	64	53	43	33	24	15
40	188	169	152	136	122	109	97	85	74	64	55	45	37	29	21	13
45	154	140	127	115	104	93	83	73	64	56	48	40	32	25	18	12
50	131	120	109	99	90	81	73	65	57	49	42	35	29	23	17	11
55	114	105	96	88	80	72	65	58	51	44	38	32	26	20	15	10
60	101	93	86	79	72	65	58	52	46	40	35	29	24	19	14	9
70	83	77	71	65	59	54	49	44	39	34	29	25	20	16	12	8
80	70	65	60	55	51	46	42	38	33	29	25	22	18	14	10	7
90	61	57	52	48	44	41	37	33	29	26	22	19	16	12	9	6
100	54	50	47	43	40	36	33	30	26	23	20	17	14	11	8	5
110	48	45	42	39	36	33	30	27	24	21	18	16	13	10	8	5
120	44	41	38	35	32	30	27	24	22	19	17	14	12	9	7	5
130	40	37	35	32	30	27	25	22	20	18	15	13	11	9	6	4
140	37	34	32	30	27	25	23	21	19	16	14	12	10	8	6	4
150	34	32	30	28	26	23	21	19	17	15	13	11	9	8	6	4
160	32	30	28	26	24	22	20	18	16	14	13	11	9	7	5	4
170	30	28	26	24	22	21	19	17	15	14	12	10	8	7	5	3
180	28	26	25	23	22	20	18	17	15	13	11	10	8	7	5	3
190	26	25	23	22	20	18	17	15	14	12	11	9	8	6	5	3

Residual Nitrogen Times (Minutes)

© International Training 2010-2013
Technical Diving International
Scuba Diving International
Emergency Response Diving International
USN SS521-AG-PRO-010 Revision 7

Item: 110520-01

** Residual Nitrogen Time cannot be determined using this table.

† Read vertically downward to the 30 fsw repetitive dive depth. Use the corresponding residual nitrogen times to compute the equivalent single dive time. Decompress using the 30 fsw air decompression table.

tdisdi.com

US Navy Air Decompression Tables

50 FSW

Bottom Time (min)	Time to First Stop (min:sec)	DECO STOP FSW 30	DECO STOP FSW 20	Total Deco Time (min:sec)	Repetitive Group
92	1:40		0	1:40	M
95	1:00		2	3:40	M
100	1:00		4	5:40	N
110	1:00		8	9:40	O
120	1:00		21	22:40	O
130	1:00		34	35:40	Z
140	1:00		45	46:40	Z
150	1:00		56	57:40	Z
160	1:00		78	79:40	Z
170	1:00		96	97:40	Z
180	1:00		111	112:40	Z
190	1:00		125	126:40	Z
200	1:00		136	137:40	Z

55 FSW

min	min:sec	30	20	min:sec	
74	1:50		0	1:50	L
75	1:10		1	2:50	L
80	1:10		4	5:50	M
90	1:10		10	11:50	N
100	1:10		17	18:50	O
110	1:10		34	35:50	O
120	1:10		48	49:50	Z
130	1:10		59	60:50	Z
140	1:10		84	85:50	Z
150	1:10		105	106:50	Z
160	1:10		123	124:50	Z
170	1:10		138	139:50	Z
180	1:10		151	152:50	Z

60 FSW

min	min:sec	30	20	min:sec	
63	2:00		0	2:00	K
65	1:20		2	4:00	L
70	1:20		7	9:00	L
80	1:20		14	16:00	N
90	1:20		23	25:00	O
100	1:20		42	44:00	Z
110	1:20		57	59:00	Z
120	1:20		75	77:00	Z
130	1:20		102	104:00	Z
140	1:20		124	126:00	Z
150	1:20		143	145:00	Z
160	1:20		158	160:00	Z

70 FSW

min	min:sec	30	20	min:sec	
48	2:20		0	2:20	K
50	1:40		2	4:20	K
55	1:40		9	11:20	L
60	1:40		14	16:20	M
70	1:40		24	26:20	N
80	1:40		44	46:20	O
90	1:40		64	66:20	Z
100	1:40		88	90:20	Z
110	1:40		120	122:20	Z
120	1:40		145	147:20	Z
130	1:40		167	169:20	Z

80 FSW

min	min:sec	30	20	min:sec	
39	2:40		0	2:40	J
40	2:00		1	3:40	J
45	2:00		10	12:40	K
50	2:00		17	19:40	M
55	2:00		24	26:40	M
60	2:00		30	32:40	N
70	2:00		54	56:40	O
80	2:00		77	79:40	Z
90	2:00		114	116:40	Z
100	1:40	1	147	150:20	Z
110	1:40	6	171	179:20	Z

90 FSW

min	min:sec	40	30	20	min:sec	
33	3:00			0	3:00	J
35	2:20			4	7:00	J
40	2:20			14	17:00	L
45	2:20			23	26:00	M
50	2:20			31	34:00	N
55	2:20			39	42:00	O
60	2:20			56	59:00	O
70	2:20			83	86:00	Z
80	2:00		5	125	132:40	Z
90	2:00		13	158	173:40	Z

100 FSW

min	min:sec	40	30	20	min:sec	
25	3:20			0	3:20	H
30	2:40			3	6:20	J
35	2:40			15	18:20	L
40	2:40			26	29:20	M
45	2:40			36	39:20	N
50	2:40			47	50:20	O
55	2:40			65	68:20	Z
60	2:40			81	84:20	Z
70	2:20		11	124	138:00	Z
80	2:20		21	160	184:00	Z

110 FSW

min	min:sec	40	30	20	min:sec	
20	3:40			0	3:40	H
25	3:00			5	8:40	I
30	3:00			14	17:40	K
35	3:00			27	30:40	M
40	3:00			39	42:40	N
45	3:00			50	53:40	O
50	3:00			71	74:40	Z
55	2:40		5	85	93:20	Z
60	2:40		13	111	127:20	Z
70	2:40		26	155	184:20	Z

120 FSW

min	min:sec	40	30	20	min:sec	
15	4:00			0	4:00	F
20	3:20			4	8:00	H
25	3:20			9	13:00	J
30	3:20			24	28:00	L
35	3:20			38	42:00	N
40	3:00		2	49	54:40	O
45	3:00		3	71	77:40	Z
50	3:00		10	85	98:40	Z
55	3:00		19	116	138:40	Z
60	3:00		27	142	172:40	Z

130 FSW

min	min:sec	40	30	20	min:sec	
12	4:20			0	4:20	F
15	3:40			3	7:20	G
20	3:40			8	12:20	I
25	3:40			17	21:20	K
30	3:20		2	32	38:00	M
35	3:20		5	44	53:00	O
40	3:20		6	66	76:00	Z
45	3:00	1	11	84	99:40	Z
50	3:00	1	20	118	143:40	Z
55	3:00	4	28	146	181:40	Z
60	3:00	12	28	170	213:40	Z

140 FSW

min	min:sec	50	40	30	20	min:sec	
10	4:40				0	4:40	E
15	4:00				5	9:40	H
20	4:00				13	17:40	J
25	3:40			3	24	31:20	L
30	3:40			7	37	48:20	N
35	3:20		2	7	58	71:00	O
40	3:20		4	7	82	97:00	Z
45	3:20		5	18	114	141:00	Z
50	3:20		8	27	145	184:00	Z
55	3:00	1	15	29	171	219:40	Z

150 FSW

min	min:sec	50	40	30	20	min:sec	
8	5:00				0	5:00	E
10	4:20				2	7:00	F
15	4:00				8	13:00	H
20	4:00			2	15	21:40	K
25	4:00			4	29	40:40	M
30	3:40		4	7	45	60:20	O
35	3:40		5	8	74	91:20	Z
40	3:20	2	6	14	106	132:00	Z
45	3:20	3	8	24	142	181:00	Z
50	3:20	4	14	28	170	220:00	Z

160 FSW

min	min:sec	60	50	40	30	20	min:sec	
7	5:20					0	5:20	E
10	4:40					4	9:20	F
15	4:20				2	10	17:00	J
20	4:00			1	4	19	28:40	L
25	4:00			4	7	35	50:40	N
30	3:40		2	6	7	62	81:20	Z
35	3:40		4	6	7	89	111:20	Z
40	3:40		6	6	21	134	171:20	Z
45	3:20	2	5	11	28	166	216:00	Z

170 FSW

min	min:sec	60	50	40	30	20	min:sec	
6	5:40					0	5:40	D
10	5:00					6	11:40	G
15	4:40				3	13	21:20	J
20	4:20			3	6	24	38:00	M
25	4:00		1	7	7	41	60:40	O
30	4:00		5	7	7	77	100:40	Z
35	3:40	2	6	6	15	120	153:20	Z
40	3:40	4	6	9	25	158	206:20	Z
45	3:40	5	7	16	28	197	257:20	Z

180 FSW

min	min:sec	70	60	50	40	30	20	min:sec	
6	6:00						0	6:00	E
10	5:20						8	14:00	H
15	4:40				2	3	14	24:20	K
20	4:20			1	5	7	29	47:00	M
25	4:20			5	7	7	57	80:00	O
30	4:00		3	6	6	7	95	121:40	Z
35	3:40	6	6	6	6	22	144	188:20	Z

190 FSW

min	min:sec	70	60	50	40	30	20	min:sec	
5	6:20						0	6:20	D
10	5:20						8	16:00	H
15	4:40				1	3	16	28:20	K
20	4:20			1	2	6	34	55:00	N
25	4:20			2	7	7	72	99:00	O
30	4:00		1	6	5	7	13	122	158:40	Z
35	4:00		4	5	6	8	26	165	218:40	Z

© International Training 2010-2013
Technical Diving International
Scuba Diving International
Emergency Response
Diving International
USN SS521-AG-PRO-010
Revision 7

v0221 Item: 110520-01

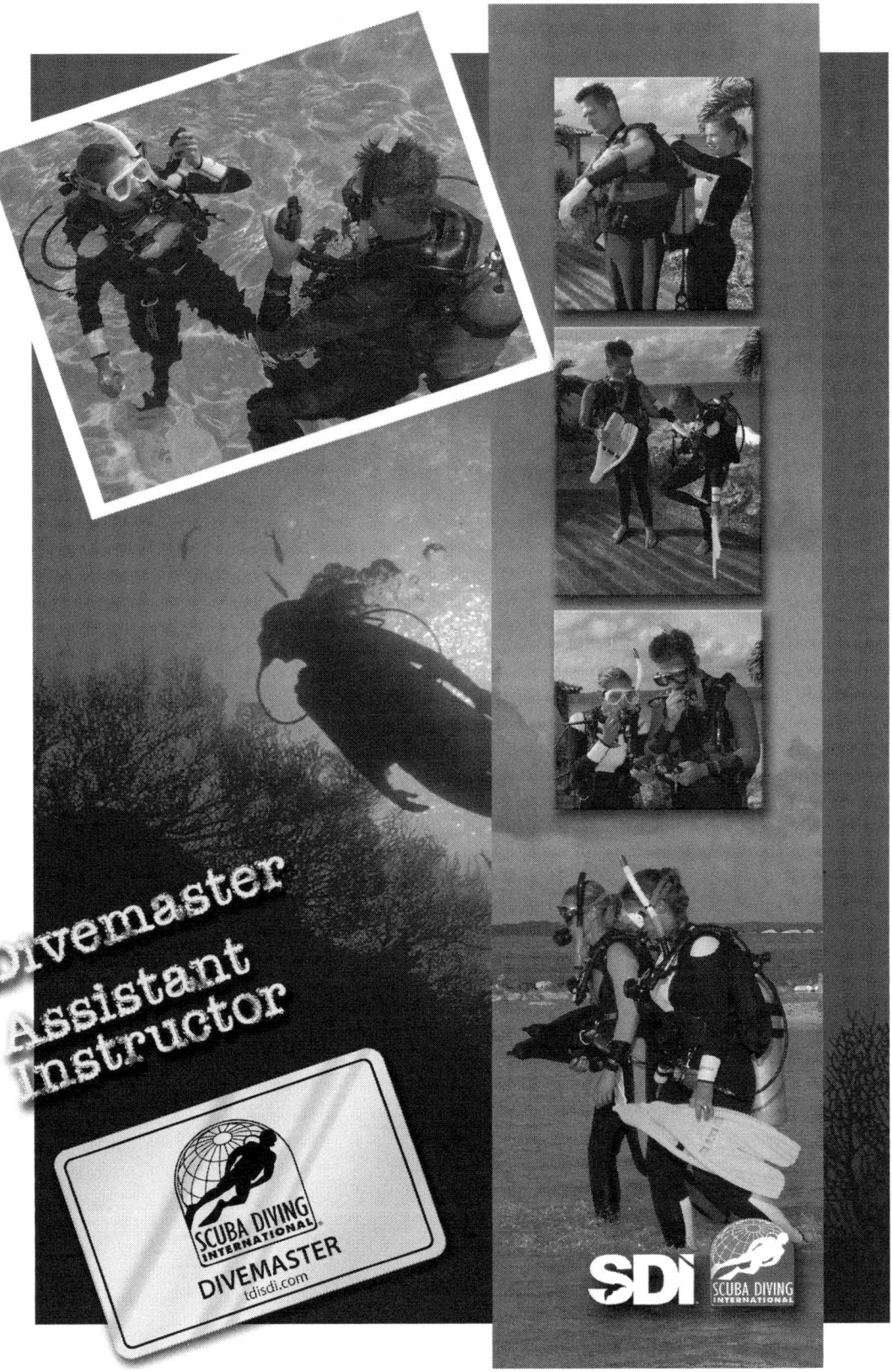

Divemaster
Assistant Instructor

APPENDIX III: An Introducton to Dive Computers

A dive computer is an electronic device that continuously monitors depth and time throughout a dive and compares this data with a theoretical model intended to duplicate how the average human body absorbs and releases nitrogen. The computer then displays the time remaining before it becomes necessary for the user to make a series of decompression stops in order to ascend safely. (Your goal is to ascend before this happens, as decompression diving entails a number of risks that are beyond the training and experience of sport divers.)

Until the late 1980s, the only way to determine what No-Decompression Limits (NDLs) to follow was to consult dive tables. Dive tables provide NDLs for various depths, depending on your depth and whether or not you have any residual nitrogen left in your system from previous dives. Dive tables have a number of limitations, including:

- They are not the easiest thing to learn to use correctly.
- Unless divers use tables on a regular basis, it is easy to forget how to use them.
- It is easy to make mistakes when using dive tables — especially as one gets older and poorer eyesight makes it easy to be off by one or more columns or rows of numbers.

Among the greatest drawbacks of dive tables is the fact they assume the deepest depth reached during a dive is the depth you were at for the entire dive. This failure to credit divers for time spent at shallower depths can severely limit available bottom time.

Dive computers help eliminate many of the problems dive tables create.

- They are easier to use.
- They are fairly reliable.
- They are not prone to making the kind of errors human beings often make when using dive tables.

- Because they continuously monitor depth and time, dive computers do not unfairly penalize divers for spending a brief portion of the dive at a deeper depth.
- Dive computers can provide additional, valuable information, such as detailed dive profiles, water temperature and ascent rate monitoring.
- When used correctly, dive computers are not only convenient, they can promote safer diving by helping control one of the most critical phases of the dive: the ascent.

Modern dive computers offer an almost dizzying array of features. These features will vary widely by make and model. Still, there are some features common to nearly all computers.

Dive Mode Features

When you take them under water dive computers enter *Dive* mode. In this mode, they will display, at a minimum:

Current Depth

Maximum Depth: The deepest you've been on this dive.

Bottom Time: The amount of time you have been under water.

No-Decompression Limit: The minutes you can remain at your current depth and still be able to ascend directly to the surface without having to make decompression stops along the way. (If you accidentally exceed this limit, your computer will tell you the depths at which you need to make decompression stops during ascent, and how many minutes to wait at each.)

Ascent Rate Warning: The mathematical model your personal dive computer uses calculates how the average human body absorbs and releases nitrogen assuming you will ascend no faster than a certain speed. When you violate this ascent rate, most computers will warn you. This usually involves a portion of the display flashing on and off, or the appearance of the word Slow, or some other indication. It's important you know what your computer's maximum ascent rate is and how the computer will warn you if you violate that ascent rate. You will want to get in the habit of CYA

Appendix III | An Introduction to Dive Computers

— Computerizing Your Ascent. That is, making your personal dive computer your primary tool for monitoring every ascent.

Surface Mode: Whenever your personal dive computer is not in Dive Mode, it will be in some form of Surface Mode. In most dive computers, there are actually several variations on Surface Mode. Surface Mode information can include several types of data, depending on make and model. The most common data include:

Surface Interval: The length of time, in hours and minutes, since you surfaced from your last dive. Your computer will continue to display this information until it assumes your body's nitrogen levels have returned to normal. (If your computer assumes you still have residual nitrogen remaining in your system from previous dives, it will shorten the No-Decompression Limit for subsequent dives.)

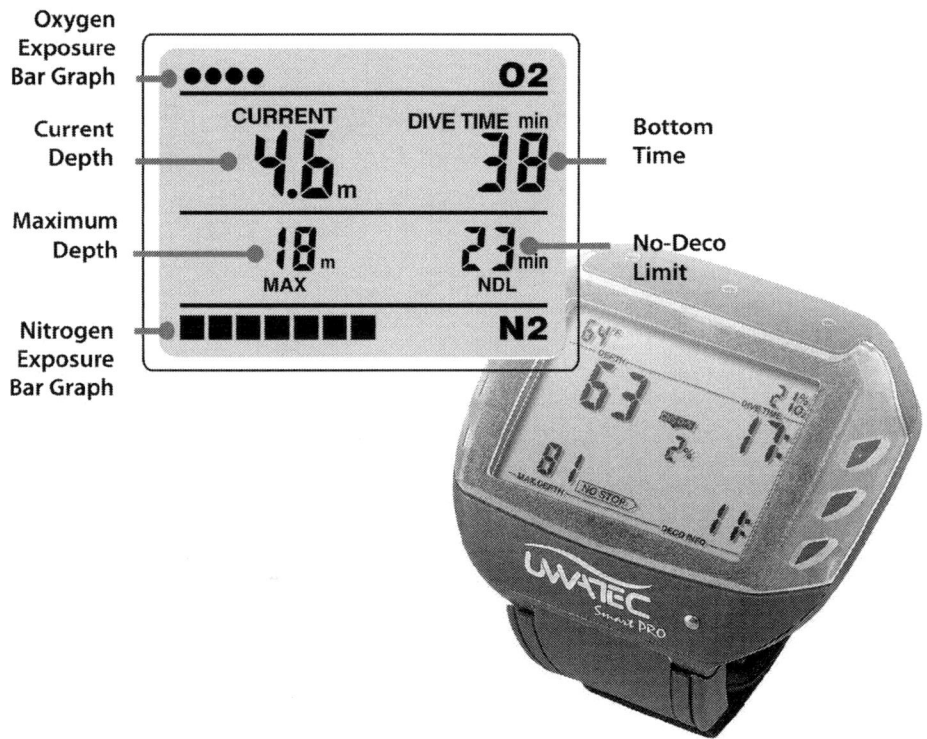

Low Battery Warning: This is exactly what the name implies — a warning that the battery is low and that you should not take the computer under water until it has been replaced. Most dive computers will not function under water if the Low Battery indicator is on.

Dive Planning: Most computers have a Dive Plan mode that will scroll the projected No-Decompression Limits for various depths, assuming you were to enter the water right now. These projections take into account any residual nitrogen the computer may assume is left in your system from previous dives.

Dive Log: In Dive Log mode, your computer will display a variety of information about previous dives, including such data as: descent/ascent times; maximum depth; actual bottom time; water temperature; and, any warnings displayed during the dive. Most dive computers can also display a dive profile — a minute-by-minute readout of exactly how deep you were at any point during the dive. Your computer's dive log capacity is limited only by its internal memory and usually covers the past several dives.

Additional Features to Look For

As mentioned earlier, most dive computers offer a dizzying array of features. Those just outlined are only the beginning. Additional features you may want to consider include:

Automatic Activation: Some early dive computers had to be turned on manually before entering the water. If you failed to do so — or if you attempted to activate the computer once you were under water — serious problems could arise. Today almost all dive computers turn on automatically as soon as you take them below the surface. This is an important safety feature and one you should not be without. Nevertheless, even though your dive computer may be capable of turning itself on under water, it's still a good idea to activate it prior to descending in order to make sure everything is functioning as it should, and that the Low Battery indicator does not appear.

PC Upload Capability: Your dive computer records depth information at intervals ranging from every minute to as little as once every few seconds. It stores this data in memory, along with information on descent/ascent time, water temperature, warnings, etc. Many dive computers have an optional PC interface that allows you to upload this data to a laptop or desktop computer, so that it will not be lost when the dive computer's internal memory fills.